Assessing Reasoning and Problem Solving

A Sourcebook for Elementary School Teachers

Stephen Krulik

Jesse A. Rudnick

Temple University

Allyn and Bacon
Boston   London   Toronto   Sydney   Tokyo   Singapore

Series editorial: Frances Helland
Series editorial assistant: Kris Lamarre
Manufacturing buyer: David Suspanic

Library of Congress Cataloging-in-Publication Data

Krulik, Stephen.
    Assessing reasoning and problem solving : a sourcebook for
elementary school teachers / Stephen Krulik, Jesse A. Rudnick.
        p.   cm.
    Includes bibliographical references.
    ISBN 0-205-19854-6
    1. Mathematics—Study and teaching (Elementary)--Evaluation.
    2. Problem solving—Study and teaching (Elementary)--Evaluation.
    I. Rudnick, Jesse A.   II. Title.
    QA135.5.K79 1998
    372.7'044--dc21   97-36967
                                                                          CIP

Printed in the United States of America
10 9 8 7 6 5 4 3 2 1   02 01 00 99 98

CONTENTS

PREFACE

During the past decade, the goals of school mathematics have been greatly expanded. Primarily due to the influence of the National Council of Teachers of Mathematics publications, *Curriculum and Evaluation Standards in School Mathematics* and *Professional Standards for Teaching Mathematics*, reasoning, problem solving, and communication skills have become major instructional objectives along with the traditional algorithmic and computational skills. As with most changes, however, these additional elements in the curriculum create a perplexing problem for classroom teachers as well as other members of the mathematics education community. How does one effectively measure the students' achievements in problem solving and reasoning? As we all know, proper assessment is needed both for diagnostic and evaluative purposes. Neither teacher-made tests nor the standardized tests traditionally used are really appropriate.

Currently, the literature abounds with ideas and suggestions for alternate assessment. The suggestions include portfolios, interviews, observations, journals, and tests utilizing various rubrics. These are all valid assessment ideas, and, taken together, form what we will call *comprehensive assessment*. What about the paper-and-pencil test? We believe that this form of assessment should still be the backbone of the teacher's schema for both evaluation and diagnostic assessment.

This book contains suggestions and materials that teachers can use to assess their students' progress in problem solving, reasoning, and communication. We have included many performance tasks and problem-specific rubrics for student analysis. With these recommendations and examples, you, the classroom teacher, will be able to ascertain the information you need to make appropriate instructional decisions as well as to establish a sound base for evaluation.

CHAPTER ONE

Assessment: The State of the Art

A large segment of the mathematics education community has favorably received the recommendations of the National Council of Teachers of Mathematics (NCTM) in the recently published *Standards*. As a result, most teachers have expanded their instructional goals to include problem solving and reasoning, along with the traditional algorithmic and computational skills. The presence of these additional elements in the curriculum, however, creates a perplexing problem for classroom teachers as well as other members of the mathematics education community. One of the current primary concerns created by the highlighting of problem solving and reasoning is how to measure the students' progress and achievement in these areas.

WHY TEACHERS ASSESS

There are two different kinds of assessment taking place in schools today: external and internal. *External assessment* usually takes the form of electronically scored examinations that are made up by some outside testing agency or state department bureau. One major purpose of these kinds of tests is simply to ascertain how schools are doing on a comparative basis within a state and how the state itself compares on a national scale. The growth of any one individual child is rarely an issue. These tests are often designed to provide legislators with an idea of how much "bang for the buck" their constituencies are getting. State Departments of Education also use these tests to determine how well school districts are meeting the state curriculum guidelines.

Local school districts use the test findings not only to compare schools within the district but also to determine how well the students, as a group, are mastering the curriculum and learning what is being taught. Some districts also use these results as a measure of teacher effectiveness.

Internal assessment, however, has a completely different set of objectives. Its main purpose is to provide a basis for instructional decisions via diagnosis. A secondary purpose is, of course, evaluative. Evaluative assessment provides information that forms the basis for a grade for a student's work. And grades *are* still important! Parents, supervisors, and school systems insist on grades—and students do value what is tested! Indeed, the most often asked question in any classroom is: Will this be on the next test?

On the other hand, the major purpose of any assessment program must be to improve learning! Diagnostic assessment permits you to analyze a student's achievement in both algorithmic and reasoning skills. This analysis provides the information on which instructional decisions regarding teaching and reteaching can be made. After all, the key to making effective instructional decisions is to base them on reasonable conclusions reached by balancing evidence across as wide an expanse of different dimensions as possible.

Students' self-assessments must also be considered within the instructional or diagnostic function. Students should be able to measure their own progress and to determine where they must place emphasis for additional experiences and effort. As the students themselves see the progress they are making, they gain a feeling of confidence in their own mathematical abilities. This inevitably leads to an increase in self-esteem and encourages them to pursue additional mathematics.

Thus, assessment must be comprehensive and assign value to *all* learning experiences, including not only conceptual understanding but also algorithmic skills, student confidence as a learner, the ability to make mathematical connections, and a general effectiveness in communicating mathematical ideas. In order to effectively assess problem solving and reasoning, you must make use of assessment tools that are sensitive to the process as well as to the end product.

HOW TEACHERS ASSESS

To almost every adult out of school, assessment meant testing! Both internal and external assessment used paper-and-pencil tests whose sole purpose was to measure achievement. In the past, external tests were designed and scored by outside sources who had only a generalized knowledge of the total student population involved. These sources designed large-scale, multiple-choice tests that concentrated mainly on algorithmic achievement. These tests were scored electronically, giving no consideration to local variations in the curriculum. The scores were then translated into national and regional norms, which were used by local agencies to ascertain the level of progress attained by their student population. The only input to the classroom teacher was a number! Unfortunately, not only was this number used to measure student placement but also to measure teacher effectiveness. It should be noted, however, that currently these outside agencies are, to some extent, adding sections to their examinations that attempt to go beyond the traditional assessment.

Internal assessment was the sole responsibility of the classroom teacher. It primarily consisted of a test given at the end of a prescribed unit of instruction. The test was constructed by the teacher, usually consisted of a set of problems taken from the content, and, in many cases, modeled after a chapter test appearing at the end of the chapter in the textbook. Credit was given for correct answers only, although partial credit was sometimes assigned. Validity and reliability were never considered. The objective was achievement of algorithmic skills. (Understand that we are not faulting teachers for this method, since no instruction in test development and scoring was ever a part of their backgrounds.) Unfortunately, this form of testing is still prominent today.

However, teachers have always gone beyond this method of testing and have made use of the additional assessment techniques of observations and questions and answers. The formal test was used to establish a grade, and, along with observation and questions and answers, helped teachers formulate their instructional strategies. In some cases, teachers incorporated this interaction with their students into the grading process.

NEED FOR A CHANGE

The testing of some traditional skills remains important; however, from the classroom level on up through the district and state levels, testing is shifting away from the multiple-choice, skill-oriented tests that have long been the trademark of the schools. Traditional testing programs were designed to find out what students did *not* know. These tests were aimed at what is probably the lowest level of mathematical development. Traditional teacher-made and standardized multiple-choice tests cannot, by themselves, provide the proper assessment of the thought processes being taught. These tests were adequate in the traditional setting, where the teacher presented a mathematical skill, explained the skill, and then allowed the students to practice the skill. Such evaluative devices focused on outcomes, but not on processes. How a student got an answer was often overlooked as long as the answer was correct. Today, educators know that the breadth and depth of a student's understanding while solving a problem cannot be determined by merely examining his or her final answer.

Teachers are currently moving more and more toward assessment that encourages students to demonstrate their thinking and conceptual knowledge in a variety of ways. Assessment must be designed that is coordinated with and parallels the instructional process. Even though it is taking time for testing agencies, school districts, and some teachers to rethink and restructure their ideas about assessment, it is clear that the nation is moving in the direction of this broader concept of assessment.

The National Council of Teachers of Mathematics, in support of its recommendations in the *Standards* that problem solving and reasoning must be the central focus of both the content and pedagogy of the mathematics classroom, has called for a number of changes in assessment practices. These modifications suggest a program of assessment that is quite different from what is currently taking place in classrooms. The following changes will be made:

From	To
Assessing what students do not know	Assessing what student know and how they think about mathematics
Having assessment be simply counting correct answers on tests for the sole purpose of assigning grades	Having assessment be an integral part of teaching
Focusing on a large number of specific and isolated skills organized by a content-behavior matrix	Focusing on a broad range of mathematical tasks and taking a holistic view of mathematics
Using exercises or word problems requiring only one or two skills	Developing problem situations that require the applications of a number of mathematical ideas
Using only written tests	Using multiple assessment techniques, including written, oral, and demonstration formats
Excluding calculators, computers, and manipulatives from the assessment process	Using calculators, computers, and manipulatives in assessment
Evaluating the program only on the basis of test scores	Evaluating the program by systematically collecting information on outcomes, curriculum, and instruction
Using standardized achievement tests as the only indicator of program outcomes	Using standardized achievement tests as only one of many indicators of program outcomes

(NCTM Curriculum and Evaluation Standards for School Mathematics, 1989, p. 191)

Current literature abounds with many suggestions for alternative forms of assessment. These include journals, portfolios, interviews, formal observations, projects, and the like. Some people are suggesting that these alternate forms of assessment should *replace* the traditional paper-and-pencil tests. We strongly disagree! We do not believe that these alternatives, by themselves, adequately determine students' growth and progress. The traditional paper-and-pencil tests still form the backbone of the teachers' schema for assessment, and we feel that these tests, together with the current suggestions, form what we shall refer to as *comprehensive assessment*.

CHAPTER TWO

Comprehensive Assessment

We divide comprehensive assessment into two major categories: ongoing tasks and snapshot tasks. *Ongoing tasks* include portfolios, journals and notebooks, and informal observations. *Snapshot tasks* include formal observations, interviews, projects, forced-choice responses (discussed in Chapter 3), and formulated responses (discussed in Chapter 4).

Assessment can be likened to a movie film. The ongoing tasks represent the entire film, whereas the snapshot tasks represent individual stills within the film. When viewed over a period of time, the two provide a comprehensive view of a student's progress.

ONGOING TASKS

The main characteristic of all ongoing tasks is that they depict a child's progress over an extended period of time—as much as a semester or even the entire academic year. For the most part, portfolios, journals, and notebooks are student productions (with some teacher input), whereas the informal observation is teacher produced.

Portfolios

When one looks at all the current writings on assessment, student portfolios have received more attention than any other single item. Although rather new to the mathematics classroom, the portfolio has been used in the performance and arts professions for many years. It is the chief method by which artists, photographers, journalists, architects, and others display their achievements. In these fields, the portfolio contains examples of an artist's best works, and is used to demonstrate proficiency and talent in his or her chosen field. It is consistently being updated to show growth.

In the mathematics classroom, the portfolio is a student-owned show-case of one's work. That is, the examples of work included in the portfolio are selected by the student, and the portfolio remains in the student's possession. In some cases, the portfolios are stored in a convenient location in the classroom. However, the basic idea behind the portfolio remains the same—it is a systematic collection of the student's best works. The portfolio permits the student to have time to think, to develop some work, and to exhibit those traits in which he or she excels. Through the use of the portfolio, the student gradually develops an idea of what is important in mathematics. The portfolio permits the student to demonstrate and observe his or her own growth and maturity in mathematics over time.

WHY USE A PORTFOLIO?   A portfolio provides a permanent and ongoing record of a student's progress. By its very nature, this ongoing record reflects lifelong learning. It provides a realistic view of the student's achievement instead of a some-times-questionable test score. It places the emphasis on what the student has accomplished rather than on any deficiencies that might exist.

Communication skills are developed and enhanced through the use of portfolios. This occurs as the students report the results of their investigations and activities. It also occurs as they continually review their inclusions.

The portfolio provides students who come from different backgrounds and who possess different learning styles with an opportunity to showcase their achievements. Above all, the portfolio provides an opportunity for students to improve their self-images by viewing the products of their own efforts.

What Goes into a Portfolio?   Obviously, students want only their best work to appear in their portfolios. Just as an artist wishes to show only his or her best works, so, too, does the student. However, it is the teacher's intention to examine the student's mathematical growth over time, as well as the student's ability to present knowledge in a variety of ways. Thus, the portfolio should contain examples of several diverse tasks, developed throughout the year. Although the student makes the final decision as to which particular works appear in the portfolio, it is the teacher (sometimes with student input) who decides what areas should be represented. Obviously, these areas should be as widely diverse as possible. Thus, the portfolio should focus on conceptual understanding, problem solving and reasoning, and communications skills. The number of items should be limited, so as not to confuse the issue with too many examples and too much extra material. The student's ability to select only the best works helps develop the metacognitive skills that educators feel are so desirable. Furthermore, the actual items selected by the student reveal what pieces of work he or she felt were most important.

The portfolio provides a marvelous opportunity for parents to keep abreast of their child's progress throughout the school year. You should be certain that the parents understand the purposes of the portfolio and periodically review the portfolio with their child. The more active the parents become, the more worthwhile the portfolio will be. This participation can form the basis for teacher/parent dialogue at future conferences.

A typical portfolio might contain several homework assignments from different time periods during the school year. That is, one assignment might come from the first few months of the school year, one from the next few months, and so on, until there are four or five homework assignments reflecting the student's growth throughout that year.

The portfolio should also contain the solutions to several problem-solving activities, especially those that the student feels are the most creative or most indicative of his or her mastery of the problem-solving process. Elegant solutions or extended analyses that show creativity and originality of thought should always be included. Students might also include any additional problems or conjectures that they have formulated as a result of their own work.

Written descriptions of practical or mathematical investigations (projects) developed over a period of time of one or two weeks are also important. These provide observers with an opportunity to see how the student works both inside and outside the class, as the investigation is developed from its initial statement of task, through the procedures decided on, to the final presentation of the results. These can be developed either individually or in small groups. When done in groups, the final report should appear in the portfolio of each student who participated in the project. This final report can be augmented by video, audio, or computer-generated materials.

The portfolio should also contain examples of anything that the student feels should be shown. Remember, the portfolio is an example of what the student considers to be his or her best work, and it should reflect this in the included selections.

Require your students to evaluate their own portfolios from time to time. For example, ask students for a Table of Contents, and then ask for a brief written description of a specific item and an explanation of why they have selected the item. Students should comment on the major strengths and weaknesses of a given product. This evaluation should also be placed in their portfolio.

Notice that we have not mentioned evaluation of a student portfolio. It is our contention that no grade should be attached to a portfolio. The portfolio has a greater purpose than for establishing a grade. It is an aid to helping students demonstrate their growth and progress over time. As such, it is more for diagnostic purposes than evaluative. The works in the portfolio, having been selected by the student as examples of his or her best efforts, are, in essence, a self-assessment made by that student. Because of this, we do not feel that a grade should be attached to what a student considers to be his or her best work. Instead, you should use the portfolio to determine to what extent your curriculum objectives have been met and how the student has grown in your mathematics class over a given period.

Journals and Notebooks

To many people, the journal and the notebook are one and the same. This may be true physically, in that both may be written in the same bound notebook, but what goes into each is quite different. The journal contains materials from the *affective* domain—feelings, opinions, and reactions. The notebook contains materials from the *cognitive* domain—homework, class notes, solutions to problems, definitions, and explanations.

Student Journals: The Affective Domain.   Journals are collections of student writings. They are introspective and reflective. The student journal enables the child to express his or her attitudes and feelings toward mathematics, the mathematics classroom, his or her own learning experiences, and how mathematics relates to his or her own world. The journal permits the child to express opinions, feelings, and reactions. It is an excellent device for accomplishing the objectives of examining student attitudes and helping students learn to write.

Student journals help students make the connections between language and mathematics. It is essential that students learn to use the language of mathematics, and journals are one way of helping them to do this. The ability to communicate in the mathematics class is critical to problem solving. A lack of communication skills might easily mask facility at solving problems, even though the student might be an excellent problem solver. The most important single way of helping your students learn to communicate is to provide opportunities for them to write in the mathematics class. Through writing, students are given the opportunity to formulate ideas, organize their thinking, internalize concepts, and evaluate the entire process.

What Goes into a Journal?   In the main, the topics about which students will write are generated by the teacher. You may wish to assign journal writing daily or only after specific lessons. Before your students write in their journals, however, you should discuss the content and the purpose of each entry that they are about to write. Encourage them to consider this as they frame their writings. These entries might include answers to such questions as:

1. What did you learn in math class today?
2. What was most challenging? Why?
3. What was easiest? Why?
4. What did you learn in math class today that you didn't know before?
5. How is what you learned today used outside of school?
6. How can *you* use what you learned outside of school?
7. How did you feel about today's lesson? Why?
8. How well do you think the class learned today's lesson?
9. How well did you learn today's lesson?
10. What did you find to be the most interesting part of the lesson? Why?
11. How did you use mathematics today, outside of school?

Some students may experience problems when they begin to write in a journal. In most cases, this will be a new experience for them. Never before have they been asked to put their thoughts and feelings into written form. Regardless, they should be encouraged to write!

We regard the student journal as a source of personal "feelings" toward mathematics on the part of the student—as a type of diary. As such, it should not be evaluated for grading purposes. The writing samples give insight into a student's feelings as well as his or her perception of your instructional efforts. This provides you with a way to determine the extent to which your goals for the entire class have been met. A major benefit to the student is a recognition of how mathematics affects his or her immediate world, every day. This will lead to an appreciation of the value and the power of mathematics.

Student Notebooks: The Cognitive Domain.   A notebook is a running inventory of a student's experiences in the mathematics classroom. It basically consists of two parts: work done at home and work done in class. In this notebook, the child includes such items as practice of algorithmic skills, definitions, explanations and models, illustrations of concepts, and solutions to problems as well as the thought processes that produced the solution.

Concepts can be illustrated with an explanation and/or a drawing. For example, to show the concept of 18 ÷ 3, the child can show two distinct models (see Figure 2.1):

Figure 2.1 The Concept of 18 ÷ 3

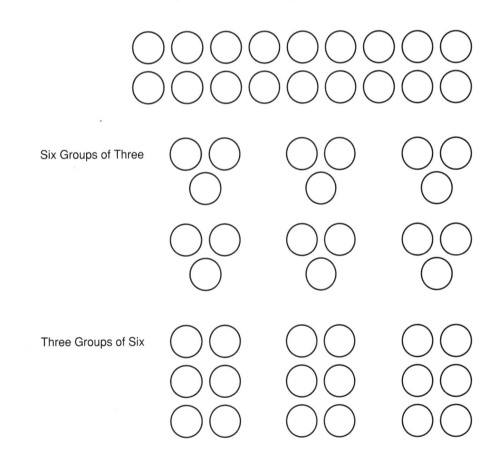

1. How many groups of 3 can be obtained from 18 objects?
2. How can 18 objects be divided into 3 equal groups?

The concept of 27% can be easily illustrated with a drawing showing a 10 × 10 square array, and shading in 27 of them. This shows that 27/100 = 27% (see Figure 2.2).

In the case of problem solving, each problem should be shown, along with its solution. When alternate solutions have been presented and discussed, they should also be shown in the notebook, together with the problem.

When problems are assigned for homework, the student's solution should be written, along with a paragraph explaining the solution and how it was achieved. This process of reviewing the thought processes that led to the solution is referred to as *metacognition*.

A Note about Metacognition.   Metacognition (thinking about one's own thinking) is an important tool for helping students become better problem solvers and reasoners. The student notebook is an excellent place to provide opportunities to utilize and to develop this important skill. Metacognition refers to one's knowledge concerning one's own cognitive processes. That is, it is the active monitoring or thinking about one's own thinking. In metacognition, the questions addressed are: What were my thoughts while I was solving this problem? and What thoughts led me to do what I did?

Some people feel that a student should be writing about his or her thinking concurrently with the actual solving of a problem, but we believe that this procedure has a tendency to disrupt the flow of ideas as the student solves the problem. Thus, we prefer that students use the technique of writing a *summative paragraph* once the problem has been solved. In effect, this would be the same information as in the metacognitive entry, but it would be written in retrospect rather than along with the actual solving of the problem.

Constructive feedback is important. You should write comments and suggestions about the entries in the notebook. These might include ques-

Figure 2.2 The Concept of 27%

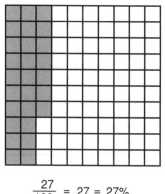

$$\frac{27}{100} = .27 = 27\%$$

tions regarding information that is not clear or ideas about other related topics that the student might wish to consider for further study. This feedback can serve as a basis for the students to review and revise their notebooks. Have students share their ideas with their classmates and brainstorm responses with their peers in a group setting before revising their notebook entries. If the notebook is to be included in the student's portfolio, the student may wish to rewrite the entries, taking into consideration the comments and suggestions made by their peers and you.

The notebook can be evaluated periodically. It should be considered in a holistic manner, and an appropriate grade assigned. This grade should be based on completeness, originality, neatness, and accuracy, and it should contribute to the student's overall mathematics grade.

Informal Observations

One obvious technique of assessment that all teachers have used over the years is observation. Observations are an integral part of the teaching process. After all, as one teaches, one is constantly observing students as they work independently and in groups, as they respond to questions, as they ask questions of their own, as they interact with their peers, and so on. There is no better way to judge the effectiveness of your teaching than to observe the children's behavior and reactions during the lesson. These observations should lead to modifications of your instructional strategy as the lesson proceeds. The main purpose of these informal observations is diagnosis rather than evaluation.

Some teachers make use of a seating chart to keep track of informal observations. They make a grid model of the classroom, using individual cells on the chart for each student. The student's name is written in the cell, and simple entries are made regularly. For example, a "+" sign might be used for a positive response, a "−" sign for a negative response, and a "?" to indicate that the student asked an outstanding question. One valuable use of this method of observation is that students who rarely take part in the class lesson will have far fewer marks in their individual cells on the grid, and this will be readily observable to the teacher at a glance.

SNAPSHOT TASKS

The main characteristic of snapshot tasks is that they reveal a child's knowledge and understanding of a given topic at a specific time. When you examine a collection of these snapshots taken cumulatively, the child's growth and progress can be clearly observed. These snapshot findings are recorded and can then be used to help determine a grade.

Formal Observations

Formal observations are particularly important when teachers wish to assess students' problem-solving process. We divide these observations into two categories: cognitive and affective. Under *cognitive*, we include how well the child uses the heuristic process and communicates his or her actions. Observation allows teachers to determine how well their students understand and utilize the heuristics of problem solving. In other words, Do they analyze the problem to determine what's going on? What are the given facts? What is the question? Do they illustrate the problem with a drawing, manipulatives, or an equation? Do they reason logically, in order to select an appropriate strategy? Once they select a strategy, do they carry it through to an answer? If a selected strategy does not work, do they give up or are they flexible enough to select a different strategy?

Now that the students have arrived at an answer, do they check for arithmetic errors? Have they answered the original question? Is their answer reasonable? Do they make generalizations? Do they extend their results to other situations? Do they attempt more than one solution? Do they ask, "What if . . . ?"

Effective communication skills allow teachers to determine the extent to which the children express their ideas clearly, both orally and in writing. Do they use appropriate mathematical language? Do they raise perceptive and penetrating questions? Can they support their solutions and clearly express how they arrived at their answer?

Observations are particularly helpful in examining the *affective* domain. What is the attitude of the children toward problem solving and mathematics, in general? Do they show patience and perseverance? Do they listen to and build on the ideas and suggestions of others? Are they well organized? Do they use time productively? Do they enter into mathematical discussions with other members of the class or the group? Are they willing to take risks, express their opinions, and carry out tasks to completion? Do they enjoy mathematics, work independently, and ask probing questions?

If you plan to use these observations to contribute to a grade, then you must document your observations. You should be able to support your conclusions drawn from the observations with actual examples of student responses. For this purpose, we recommend using a form similar to the one found in Figure 2.3 and in Reproduction Page 1. Complete the form either during or immediately after class, and then place it in the student's folder. Although this task may appear to be overwhelming, the use of this form will help simplify your work. Do not attempt to formally observe more than one or two students in any single day. Rather, spread the observations out over a period of one to two weeks so that every student is observed. This should be done on a regular basis.

Interviews

Interviewing students can present a rich source of information regarding their thought processes. The interview provides an opportunity for you and your students to meet on a one-on-one basis. Students who might have some trouble reading (especially younger students) can respond verbally in an interview, enabling you to assess their thought processes and their abilities to reason while problem solving. With paper-and-pencil tasks, students' understandings may often be hidden.

An interview requires you to prepare a planned sequence of questions to ask the students. You might decide to pose a problem for the students to solve at the interview, verbalizing their thoughts as they proceed through

Figure 2.3 Observation Assessment Form

Student's Name ⎯⎯⎯⎯⎯⎯⎯⎯⎯⎯⎯ Date ⎯⎯⎯⎯

OBSERVATION ASSESSMENT FORM

0 = Inadequate   1 = Satisfactory   2 = Good   3 = Exemplary

Category	0	1	2	3	Illustrations
Understands the Problem Facts, questions; illustrates by means of manipulatives, drawings, etc.					
Selects a Plan Appropriate strategy; alternative strategy.					
Carries Out the Plan Carries out strategy; arrives at an answer; effectively does work; carefully organized.					
Reflect Checks computation; reasonableness; answers the question; extends the problem.					
Communication Expresses ideas clearly; orally and/or written; uses appropriate mathematical language; asks appropriate questions.					
Attitude Patience; perseverance; uses time productively; willing to take risk; enjoys problem solving.					

the solution process. By listening to a student's thoughts about the problem, and observing his or her use of diagrams, drawings, or models, you will gain insight into the meanings and understandings that the student has assigned to particular procedures and concepts. You will also gain insight into the student's confidence level, attitude toward mathematics, and work habits when engaged in problem solving. You can also assess his or her ability to communicate mathematical knowledge verbally.

Although interviews are, of necessity, quite time consuming, they often yield depth and quality about a student's work that might not be revealed via a pencil-and-paper test. They are also an excellent tool for diagnosing the individual needs of a student who is experiencing difficulties in problem solving. The questions that the students ask themselves while attempting to resolve a problem they have been given are a significant source of information about their problem-solving abilities. If they have currently internalized the problem-solving process they have been taught, you should hear them asking such questions as:

- What is this problem about?
- What am I asked to find?
- What facts am I given? Are there any facts missing?
- What is a good place to start?
- What is a good strategy to try? Why did I choose this strategy?
- What's a good next step?
- What do I still need to know?
- Have I answered the given question?
- Is there another way to attack this problem?

Although you should have a general plan for questioning during the interview, the actual questions you ask will depend on the student's responses as the interview progresses. The key here is flexibility!

You should plan the interview in advance. If carefully structured, each interview may take only 5 to 10 minutes. Since most students attach a great deal of importance to an interview, you may wish to assure them that they all will be interviewed at some time during the year. You may decide to schedule one or two interviews each week.

Inform the students where and when the interviews will take place. Clearly clarify that the interview is intended to provide the opportunity for the student and teacher to interact in a nonthreatening atmosphere. Explain that you will be looking at their thought processes, and will do this by having them solve a problem while thinking out loud, explaining as much as they can. You may also inform the students that you will be taking some notes so as not to forget any interesting or important things that they say.

During the interview, while the student is solving the problem, you should take some brief notes. However, be aware that taking written notes may prove to be upsetting to some students and might destroy the spontaneity of their responses. Here, you may have to rely primarily on mental notes to be transcribed immediately after the interview is concluded. You should be a good listener and be nonjudgmental about the students' responses. If you feel the need to prompt, do so, but minimally. Be careful not to interpret nor teach. Avoid cuing and leading the children. Do not interrupt—let the students' thoughts flow freely. Remember, your goal is to find out where each child is in terms of problem-solving concepts and procedures. Always begin and end the interview on a positive, upbeat note.

When the interview has been concluded, write down your notes carefully and summarize the results. You may wish to use the interview form shown in Figure 2.4 and Reproduction Page 2. Do not assume that you will be able to remember everything that has happened during the interview at a later time Date your notes and place them into the student's folder. Use them to make changes in your own teaching if necessary. Remember that an interview allows you to meet with your students on an informal basis—one that permits them to think freely on a highly cognitive level, often beyond what you might have expected, based on their other classroom experiences and performances. Interviewing is not easy, but the rewards of listening to your students are great.

Projects

For many years, projects were not often assigned in the mathematics classroom. In a skill-oriented curriculum, projects did not play much of a role. Students simply practiced a skill immediately after it had been taught. Now, however, with the increased focus on problem solving and reasoning, projects play a significant role for every student. Projects should be included in the mathematics program and should also be a part of comprehensive assessment. Generally, projects present students with a real-life problem or situation, and challenge them to use their mathematics skills and knowledge to resolve it. Projects offer a viable way to focus on such NCTM *Standards* as students undertaking real-life problem solving, communicating mathematically, and using technology as a tool in mathematics. In addition, projects are excellent ways to have students reinforce the use of their knowledge, skills, and concepts outside of the mathematics classroom.

Projects can be carried out by individuals or can be assigned to small, cooperative learning groups of three or four students. This latter format helps students sharpen their communication skills as they talk with the members of their group. Projects are not short assignments; rather, they should involve an ongoing task that takes about two to three weeks. They provide a wonderful means for involving students in extended problem-solving situations. The situations should be mathematical in nature, and relate directly to the real world. This enables the students to see a real-world connection to their mathematics courses. In addition, the themes of projects can often integrate mathematics with other school subjects. Projects may be open ended and have a variety of acceptable results. They may be such that they lead the students to make further conjectures. Projects that are embedded in a problem-solving content can be used to help students explore, study, and pursue ideas that develop their understanding of mathematics as a living, necessary subject.

Projects also encourage communication, as students interact with other students and write clear descriptions of the project. This might take

Figure 2.4 Interview Assessment Form

Student's Name ———————————————— Date ————

INTERVIEW ASSESSMENT FORM

0 = Inadequate   1 = Satisfactory   2 = Good   3 = Exemplary

Category	0	1	2	3	Illustrations
Understands the Problem Facts, questions; illustrates by means of manipulatives, drawings, etc.					
Selects a Plan Appropriate strategy; alternative strategy.					
Carries Out the Plan Carries out strategy; arrives at an answer; effectively does work; carefully organized.					
Reflect Checks computation; reasonableness; answers the question; extends the problem.					
Communication Expresses ideas clearly; orally and/or written; uses appropriate mathematical language; asks appropriate questions.					
Attitude Patience; perseverance; uses time productively; willing to take risk; enjoys problem solving.					

the form of simple statements or questions that must be resolved. School projects should parallel real life in that real life involves recognizing that the problem exists. *Being able to clearly formulate the problem is, in itself, an ideal problem-solving task.* In the real world, problems are rarely well defined; projects will help develop this much needed skill. Students must define the problem, set the parameters for what is to be done, decide how to do it, assign specific tasks to group members (when appropriate), and carry out the work. The results must then be coordinated and presented in class in a clear, succinct, and appropriate format. This presentation should be done both orally and in written format.

Above all, a project must be feasible, interesting to the students, and capable of providing them with experiences designed to help them grow mathematically. In addition, there are outcomes that occur as a result of working on a project that may not always be mathematical. For example, students should learn that real-world problems are not always simple and easy to resolve in a short period of time. They should learn how to plan, organize, and pursue long-terms goals. Learning to work with other students on a project is another important outcome. And finally, the ability to write a careful, concise, and complete report, as well as present the material orally, are all critical skills needed later on in life.

But how does the project fit into the overall assessment picture? How does a teacher evaluate a project? First of all, you can examine the basic steps that the students have taken in designing their project. Have they clearly defined the problem? If so, then the key mathematical concepts and ideas should be readily apparent. The procedures that have been used to investigate and/or resolve the situation reveal how logically the children have carried through the project. The collection of the data, its organization, and its analysis all provide evidence of problem solving and reasoning. The selection of appropriate techniques to represent or model the material (i.e., drawings, graphs, equations, etc.) serve to demonstrate an understanding of mathematical connections. Finally, the written record of the results and the oral presentations should provide you with further insight into the students' thinking.

Assessment of the project can follow the format that we have previously discussed under Formal Observations and Interviews. The student's efforts can be divided into three categories: design, implementation, and presentation. The same 0–3 numerical scale can be used. Figure 2.5 and Reproduction Page 3 present such a form. (*Note*: A series of specific suggestions for projects will be found in Chapter 5, later in this book.)

Performance Tasks

A performance task is a problem or project assigned to a student or group of students that challenges them to demonstrate their mathematical power. In other words, the performance task enables children to show what they know and how well they can use what they know. The students must resolve the problem and support their solution. These are teacher-made assignments and have always been the teacher's responsibility.

The tasks must be meaningful and thought provoking to the child, permitting him or her to display understanding and thinking. They should

Figure 2.5 Project Assessment Form

Student's Name ———————————————— Date ————

PROJECT ASSESSMENT FORM

0 = Inadequate   1 = Satisfactory   2 = Good   3 = Exemplary

Category	0	1	2	3	Illustrations
Design Clearly defines the problem; key mathematical ideas apparent; procedures logical; sets reasonable parameters.					
Implementation Data collected carefully; tasks divided reasonably; carried out in logical fashion.					
Presentation Data organized and analyzed; findings presented carefully, logically, via an appropriate method (drawings, graphs, etc.); oral presentation clear; written presentation clear; resolves the problem or situation.					

also be varied—some can be resolved in a relatively short period of time, while others may extend over several days. Ideally, the task should raise other questions and lead to other problems. Above all, it should stimulate the child to perform at his or her maximum capability. Regardless of the specifics, *the performance task requires that the child perform!*

Using performance tasks offers many advantages for the teacher, the students, as well as the parents. First of all, performance tasks are an integral, natural part of instruction; they do not *interrupt* instruction. Second, projects, extended solutions to problems, and realistic tasks can be included that will enable the students to see how mathematics affects them over time. Parents are able to see evidence that their children can think and use mathematics in situations that connect school to their world. Finally, performance tasks provide a window through which teachers can observe the students' understanding of mathematics and their abilities to use mathematics in practical situations.

It is particularly important to the students that teachers assign performance tasks, since these provide the students with the opportunity to demonstrate their understanding of the processes as well as the use of algorithmic skills. It also permits them to realize the importance of mathematics in their daily lives, and that mathematics encompasses more than merely memorizing a series of unrelated rules. The nonroutine problems that we include in this book are, in essence, performance tasks.

How does a teacher assess a child's thought processes from his or her performance? In the past, teachers were concerned with the algorithmic skills used to solve the problems. However, with the additional emphasis now being placed on problem solving and reasoning, a more in-depth examination of the child's problem-solving process becomes necessary, both for diagnostic and evaluative purposes. In previous sections, we have discussed how observations, interviews, and projects can assist you in this task. A currently advocated scoring device that facilitates this is known as a *rubric*.

RUBRICS   A rubric is a schema that assists teachers in assessing a child's solution to a problem, based on several preset criteria. Teachers have always given partial credit but rarely stated the basis for how the grade was given. By setting these criteria in advance, the assigning of partial credit is formalized. This change provides teachers with evidence to support a given grade. A rubric explains how work will be evaluated. Thus, it alerts the children not only to what is expected of them as they present their solutions but also to the difference between the various scoring levels. It is commonly accepted that students perform better on a task if they are aware of exactly what it is they are expected to do.

Solutions to a problem can be assessed in two ways: holistically or analytically. In both cases, however, the difference between achievement levels must be clearly stated. In *holistic scoring*, a single grade is awarded to the student based on an overall judgment of the completed product or performance. In *analytic scoring*, a set of grades is given, each based on an individual category. These may then be combined to arrive at a single score or grade. Analytic scoring not only provides the teacher with the evidence needed to determine and support a grade but it can also provide a diagnostic profile for each student. For each problem to be assessed, a rubric should be created that reflects the specific important characteristics of that problem.

Holistic Rubrics.   A holistic rubric permits a reader to view a student's performance as a whole. That is, the rubric describes the criteria for achieving different levels of performance. Typically, four or five performance levels are summarized in some detail, with a number from 0 to 4 assigned to each level. A teacher, after reading the student's product, assigns a value for the performance, based on the quality of the overall response. The holistic rubric should be used mainly for evaluation; it has little diagnostic value. Figure 2.6 (also Reproduction Page 4) is an example of a holistic rubric.

This sample holistic rubric contains general criteria for each achievement level. In order to achieve a score of 4, the student must exhibit in his

Figure 2.6 Holistic Rubric

Student's Name ──────────────── Date ───────

HOLISTIC RUBRIC

Problem Number ──────   Score: ── ── ── ── ──
                                    4   3   2   1   0

CRITERIA

4 *Excellent*
The student has:
    selected an appropriate strategy; and
    obtained a correct and complete answer; and
    presented a logical explanation.

3 *Good*
The student has:
    selected an appropriate strategy, implemented it correctly, but made
    a minor computational error; or
    made a minor interpretive error, but obtained a correct answer
    based on the interpretation.

2 *Minimally Satisfactory*
The student has:
    answered only part of the problem; or
    made a major computational or conceptual error; or
    selected an appropriate strategy, but did not carry it through.

1 *Inadequate*
The student has:
    indicated the correct data, but has done no work; or
    given a correct answer without work.

0 *No attempt*
The student has:
    given no response; or
    given an irrelevant response.

or her work *all* of the criteria shown. However, to obtain a score of 0, 1, 2, or 3, the student need only exhibit any one of the criteria listed. Notice that, as written, the individual criteria may be open to interpretation. In order to make the criteria more definitive, the characteristics to be examined in each category should be established specifically for the problem to which the rubric is being applied.

We are not including any specific problem scored holistically. As we have said before, holistic scoring contributes little to diagnosis. Furthermore, proper use of the analytic rubric can provide a score that is equivalent to the score obtained holistically.

Analytic Rubrics.   The analytic rubric enables us to analyze the problem-solving process utilized by the child in carrying out a performance task. This is in contrast to the holistic rubric, which looks at the student's performance only as an entity. In the analytic rubric, the student's achievement level in each of the categories emphasized in the classroom instruction can be examined separately. The rubric helps point out the areas in which a particular child needs additional experiences, as well as those in which he or she is doing well. It also helps direct further instruction.

The analytic rubric is divided into categories that are the emphasis of problem-solving instruction. The categories in this rubric are based on the heuristics developed in our earlier book, *Reasoning and Problem Solving: A Handbook for Elementary School Teachers* (Allyn and Bacon, 1995). These categories include "Understands the problem," "Selects a plan, and "Carries out the plan." We have added a fourth category—namely, "Communicates the solution"—that will include the "Look back" of the original heuristics. Examining this category enables the teacher to assess the student's ability to convey his or her thoughts about the problem and its solution. Obviously, communication skills will affect each of the other categories, since it is only through communication skills that teachers are able to examine students' thought processes. The student must not only read and interpret the requirements of the task at hand but must also express his or her mathematical knowledge and thoughts in written form. Thus, a deficiency may occur, not because of a lack of knowledge, but because of a lack of the ability to communicate this knowledge. In the extreme case, the inability of a student to communicate can completely obscure his or her ability to reason, even though this ability might be significant. With such students, additional assessment techniques such as observations and interviews are necessary.

We have also added another category, called "Creativity." This provides an opportunity for the teacher to recognize original and unique thinking on the part of the student. This should not be included in the summative score, but it at least serves to indicate a creative mind, which should be acknowledged and rewarded. Teachers should always be looking for signs of creativity in students and encouraging growth in this area. This added item in the rubric enables teachers to provide the recognition of creativity when it occurs.

Notice that when a holistic score or grade is desired, it can be obtained by summing the scores from each of the four major categories and obtaining their average. (*Note*: We have chosen to use a 5-point [0–4] scale on the holistic rubric and a 4-point [0–3] scale on the analytic rubric. A conversion table can be developed if you wish to equate your findings.) Figure 2.7 (also Reproduction Page 5) shows a generic analytic rubric. It will be necessary for you to examine each problem to determine the characteristics specific to that problem. This is similar to what teachers have always done in the past, when assigning partial credit. It is often necessary to examine the child's entire solution to find the places where he or she has met the specific characteristics. In other words, understanding of the problem might be demon-

Figure 2.7 Analytic Rubric

Student's Name _____ Date _____

ANALYTIC RUBRIC

Characteristics	Criteria	Score
Understands the Problem a. Illustrates the problem with a drawing, table, equation, etc. b. Identifies the necessary data or information c. Identifies the question to be answered	3 = a, b, and c 2 = any 2 of a, b, or c 1 = any 1 of a, b, or c 0 = no meaning-ful responses	
Selects a Plan a. Selects appropriate strategy and initiates implementation b. Selects appropriate strategy with no implementation or initiates implementation of a questionable strategy c. Inappropriate strategy selected and not implemented d. No meaningful plan shown	3 = a only 2 = b only 1 = c only 0 = d	
Carries Out the Plan Implements plan and shows: a. Correct answer with appropriate work b. Appropriate work with minor computational or interpretation error c. Major interpretative or computational error d. No meaningful response	3 = a only 2 = b only 1 = c only 0 = d	
Communicates the Solution a. Gives the correct answer and a complete, logical explanation of how it was achieved, using appropriate mathematical vocabulary b. Work is neatly and carefully presented with the answer labeled c. Tables and/or diagrams are clearly labeled	3 = a, b, and c 2 = any 2 of a, b, or c 1 = any 1 of a, b, or c 0 = no work shown	
Creativity a. Unusual or unique solution given b. More than one solution c. A generalization	1 = a or b or c	

Figure 2.8 Student Profiles

	Problem #1	Problem #2	Problem #3	Problem #4	Total
Eric					
Understands	3	3	3	3	12
Selects	3	3	3	3	12
Carries out	3	3	2	3	11
Communicates	3	3	3	3	12
Creativity	-	-	1	-	1
Total	12	12	11 +1	12	47 +1
Michelle					
Understands	2	3	3	2	10
Selects	1	2	2	1	6
Carries out	2	3	3	3	11
Communicates	3	3	1	3	10
Creativity	-	-	-	-	-
Total	8	11	9	9	37
William					
Understands	3	3	3	3	12
Selects	3	2	3	1	9
Carries out	3	2	0	1	6
Communicates	3	2	2	3	10
Creativity	-	-	-	-	-
Total	12	9	8	8	37
Louise					
Understands	3	3	3	3	12
Selects	3	3	3	3	12
Carries out	3	2	3	2	10
Communicates	1	1	3	1	6
Creativity	1	-	1	-	2
Total	10 +1	9	12 +1	9	40 +2
Antoinette					
Understands	0	3	0	0	3
Selects	0	3	1	0	4
Carries out	0	3	0	0	3
Communicates	0	3	0	0	3
Creativity	-	-	-	-	-
Total	0	12	1	0	13

strated by the way in which the child indicates his or her answer, lists correct units, and so on.

The most advantageous characteristic of the analytic rubric is that, taken over time, it can relay to the teacher the child's development in each phase of the problem-solving process. It provides a visual profile of the child's progress.

Figure 2.8 shows a profile of five students. The information shown was collected by the analytic rubric, used to assess four problems over time. What does it reveal? Obviously, Eric is a star student. He received 47 out of a possible 48 points and he shows extreme competence in each category. However, he shows only minimal creativity. Perhaps Eric ought to be given more challenging experiences and be encouraged to be more creative. He could be asked to supply alternate solutions and to extend a problem whenever possible.

Notice that Michelle and William both received the same total score of 37. Yet the profile reveals that their weaknesses occur in two very different places. Michelle needs additional experiences with strategy selection, whereas William needs more practice in the algorithmic skills.

Further examination of the profile clearly indicates the strengths and needs of other individual students. Antoinette, for example, presents an interesting case. When she understands the problem (see Problem #2 column), she does well. However, in the other problems, her lack of understanding (or lack of communication skills?) prevents her from achieving.

Periodically throughout the school year, the generic analytic rubric should be discussed with the children. Since each category is an integral part of the problem-solving heuristics, this discussion will reinforce the entire problem-solving process as well as remind the students of the criteria by which they will be evaluated. In fact, it is important for the students to be involved in determining the specific characteristics of a rubric. When the child examines a problem to determine the specific characteristics used in scoring, he or she gains a deeper insight into the problem and its various solutions. This obviously results in an increased depth of understanding. After the students have completed their solutions, a discussion can ensue to determine these specific characteristics. Practically speaking, student participation in this manner is not always possible. However, when students are involved, the result is a marvelous learning experience. It also helps them to see how their final scores were achieved.

In Chapter 4, we will illustrate the use of the problem-specific, analytic rubric in much greater detail.

CHAPTER THREE

Forced-Choice Questions

Tests that contain forced-choice questions (usually referred to as multiple-choice or true-false tests) have always been the mainstay of external tests. These questions are more difficult to develop than those commonly used on tests made by teachers for use in their own classes. However, they are more easily scored, usually electronically or with an answer grid or template. The primary function of these tests, in most cases, is to measure the achievement levels the students have attained in computation and other algorithmic skills.

Most teachers are familiar with these multiple-choice or forced-choice questions. Each question contains a stem followed by several options or choices. The student is to select the correct answer from among the options provided. The general objection to these questions has been that they usually reveal only the final result, and reveal nothing about the child's thought processes. The selection of a correct answer may involve only recognition or simple recall.

From an instructional point of view, these tests are of little value to you, the teacher. In fact, in most cases, all you will receive is a score, if anything at all. The tests are primarily used to determine where the child, the class, the school, or the district lies on a standardized, comparative scale. In those limited number of cases where the tests are returned, a correct response may even lead you to an erroneous conclusion. For example, consider the following forced-choice item:

1. 60% of 20 is:
   a. less than 20
   b. equal to 20
   c. more than 20
   d. cannot be determined

A student may know that 60% = .6, and think that, since .6 is less than 20, he or she should select choice (a). Although this is indeed the correct answer, the student obviously does not understand the concept/skill that the question is attempting to examine.

In spite of their shortcomings, we believe these tests should be constructed and used in your classroom. First of all, they provide students with experience in taking tests similar to those that will confront them throughout their lives. Second, they are a good way to ascertain the progress the students have made in mastering algorithmic skills.

But can these forced-choice questions help in the teaching and learning of problem solving? Yes, they can. It is possible to design forced-choice questions that will enable you to assess a child's progress and achievement in parts of the problem-solving process. The questions can help you diagnose errors as the child proceeds through the solution of a problem, thus permitting you to make instructional adjustments. You can design questions that have the students identify the question being asked, identify the facts of the problem, determine sufficiency of data (i.e., extra information or missing information), and even determine the meaning of the key ideas of the problem. You can even use forced-choice questions to determine which strategy the student feels is the most appropriate for a certain problem.

In this chapter, you will find forced-choice questions that you can use with your students as part of your instruction and assessment of problem solving and reasoning. These should also serve as models from which you can develop additional, similar questions appropriate to your own students. We recognize that this is a formidable task, but we feel strongly that the results warrant the effort. Furthermore, once the forced choice has been selected and discussed, each problem should be solved by the students.

WHAT'S THE QUESTION?

The focal point of every problem is the question being asked. The question itself is not always obvious; nor is it necessarily indicated by a question mark. For younger children, in particular, identifying the question may be a challenge. Classroom time should be devoted to having children identify *What's the Question?* After all, if the student does not know what to find, not much can take place.

In the following pages, we have included forced-choice questions designed to provide practice in identifying the question being asked. These questions are for grades 2 through 6. We have not included grades 7 and 8 because, by this time, the students should have had sufficient experience in this activity. Similarly, grades K and 1 have been omitted due to the reading levels. However, this is not to minimize the importance of the activity even at these grade levels; practice should be carried out verbally on a regular basis, as a class activity. In each Reproduction Page (at the back of this book), have the students circle the letter of the correct choice. Then discuss this with the class. Finally, once the question has been determined, have all the problems solved.

GRADE 2   (Reproduction Pages 6 and 7)

1. Mrs. Miller wants to give 2 T-shirts to each of her 6 grandchildren. The T-shirts cost $4.00 each. How many T-shirts must she buy?

   What's the Question?
   a. How many grandchildren does Mrs. Miller have?
   b. How many T-shirts will she give each child?
   *c. How many T-shirts does she need?
   d. How much did she spend for the T-shirts?
   (Answer: She must buy 12 T-shirts.)

2. There are 3 boys and 4 girls swimming in the lake. There are 6 girls in canoes. There are 4 boys in rowboats. Find the number of children in boats.

   What's the Question?
   a. How many children are swimming?
   b. How many boys are at the lake?
   c. How many girls are in boats?
   *d. How many children are in canoes and rowboats?
   (Answer: There are 10 children in the boats.)

3. There are 12 cookies, 10 pies, 8 cakes, and 5 muffins for sale at the school fair. How many muffins and cakes are for sale?

   What's the Question?
   a. How many cookies are for sale?
   *b. How many cakes and muffins are for sale?
   c. How many things are for sale?
   d. How many more pies than muffins are for sale?
   (Answer: There are 13 cakes and muffins for sale.)

4. Antonio has 7 baseball cards left. Find how many cards he started with if he gave 2 cards to Julia and 5 cards to Marian.

   What's the Question?
   *a. How many baseball cards did Antonio start with?
   b. How many baseball cards did Antonio give to Julia?
   c. How many baseball cards did Antonio give to Marian?
   d. How many baseball cards did Antonio have left?
   (Answer: Antonio started with 14 cards.)

GRADE 3   (Reproduction Pages 8 and 9)

1. Amanda and Ian collect toy cars. Ian has 3 more cars than Amanda. Together they have 21 cars. How many cars does Amanda have in her collection?

   What's the Question?
   a. How many cars does Ian have?
   b. How many more cars has Ian than Amanda?
   c. How many cars must Amanda get to have the same number as Ian?
   *d. How many cars does Amanda have altogether?
   (Answer: Amanda has 9 cars.)

2. Antoinette and Martin are the teacher assistants in class today. They are giving out the crayons in class. They distribute 144 crayons evenly among the 24 children in the room. How many crayons did each child receive?

   What's the Question?
   a. How many crayons did Antoinette and Martin give out altogether?
   b. How many children were in the room?
   c. How many crayons did Antoinette and Martin receive?
   *d. How many crayons was each child given?
   (Answer: Each student received 6 crayons.)

3. Mrs. Carlyle and her scout troop are involved in an environmental project this month. Gwen and her two girlfriends collected aluminum cans for the month, then took them to the recycling center where they received $24, which they divided equally among themselves. How much did each girl get from the recycling center?

   What's the Question?
   a. How much money did the girls receive altogether?
   *b. How much money did each of the three girls receive?
   c. How many girls are in Mrs. Carlyle's troop?
   d. How many cans did Gwen and her friends collect?
   (Answer: Each girl received $8.)

4. The local grocery store sold apples at 5 for 95¢, or 20¢ each. How much do you save when you buy five apples at a time?

   What's the Question?
   a. How much does one apple cost?
   b. How much do five apples cost?
   *c. How much do you save if you buy five apples at a time?
   d. How many apples does the store sell?
   (Answer: You save 5¢.)

GRADE 4   (Reproduction Pages 10 and 11)

1. There are 36 students in Mrs. Johnson's class. She wishes to form teams of 8 students each. Find the number of students left after all the teams are chosen.

   What's the Question?
   *a. How many students are not placed on a team?
   b. How many students are in the class?
   c. How many students will be on each team?
   d. How many teams will there be in each class?
   (Answer: There will be 4 students left.)

2. The temperature is rising at a constant rate of 3 degrees each hour. In how many hours will the temperature be at 21 degrees if it is now 6 degrees?

What's the Question?
a. What is the temperature at the end of 3 hours?
b. How many hours will it be until the temperature goes up 21 degrees?
*c. How many hours will it be until the temperature reaches 21 degrees?
d. How many degrees does the temperature change in 1 hour?
(Answer: In 5 more hours the temperature will reach 21 degrees.)

3. During her spring break, Mandy decided to read a historical novel. There were 485 pages in the book. On the first day, she read 162 pages. On the second day, she read 85 pages, and on the next day, she read 160 pages. How many pages remain to be read?

   What's the Question?
   a. How many pages did Mandy read?
   b. How many pages did Mandy read on the first two days?
   *c. How many pages are still left to be read after the third day?
   d. How many pages does the novel contain?
   (Answer: Mandy has 78 more pages to read.)

4. A case of paper towels contains 24 rolls and costs the dealer $22.80. He sells each roll for $1.25. How much profit does he make on each roll?

   What's the Question?
   a. How much profit does he make on each case?
   *b. How much profit does he make on each roll?
   c. How much does each roll cost the dealer?
   d. How much does the dealer pay for a case of towels?
   (Answer: He makes a profit of 30¢ on each roll.)

GRADE 5   (Reproduction Pages 12 and 13)

1. Jenny bought a 36-picture roll of film for $4.00. She then paid $8.80 to have the film processed. What was the cost of each print she kept, if 4 of the pictures were underexposed and she threw them away?

   What's the Question?
   a. What was the cost of the film?
   b. What was the cost of processing the film?
   *c. What was the cost of each good picture?
   d. How much did Jenny spend altogether?
   (Answer: The cost of each good picture was 40¢.)

2. Mario and Joanne each bought the exact same car. Mario decided to have power seats and a CD player installed as extras. The power seats cost him $480. Find the cost of the CD player if Joanne paid $18,570 for her car, while Mario paid $19,450 for his.

   What's the Question?
   a. How much did Mario pay for his power seats?

b. How much did Mario pay for his car?

c. How much more did Mario pay for his car than Joanne paid for hers?

*d. How much did Mario pay for the CD player?

(Answer: The CD player cost Mario $400.)

3. The Garcia family was driving from Boston, Massachusetts, to Richmond, Virginia. It took them 4 hours to drive the 200 miles from Boston to New York, where they stopped for lunch. They then drove from New York to Philadelphia, a distance of 110 miles in 2 hours, and from Philadelphia to Washington, 150 miles, where they stopped for dinner. Then they continued on for the final 100 miles to Richmond. How far had they driven when they stopped for dinner?

What's the Question?

a. What was the length of the trip?

b. How long did the trip take them?

*c. How far had they driven from Boston to Washington?

d. How far did they drive after dinner?

(Answer: They had driven 460 miles.)

4. A 16-inch pizza is cut into 8 equal slices. The pizza contains 3,400 calories and costs $12.60. Four friends shared the pizza equally. Find the number of calories in each slice.

What's the Question?

a. How many slices did each person eat?

b. How much did each person pay?

c. How many calories did each person eat?

*d. How many calories are in each slice of the pizza?

(Answer: There are 425 calories in each slice of the pizza.)

GRADE 6   (Reproduction Pages 14 and 15)

1. There are 5 players on the defensive line of the Bearcats football team. Their average weight is 274 pounds. Joe Blue weighs 260 pounds, Marcus Saunders weighs 274 pounds, Orin Chennin weighs 289 pounds, and Leonard Rye weighs 281 pounds. Find the weight of the fifth linesman, Darrin McCoy.

What's the Question?

a. What is the weight of the heaviest player on the defensive line?

b. What is the weight of the lightest player on the defensive line?

*c. What is the weight of the fifth player on the defensive line?

d. What is the average weight of the 5 players on the defensive line?

(Answer: Darrin McCoy weighs 266 pounds.)

2. Arlene is buying beef for a local butcher shop. She paid $1.25 a pound for a side of beef that weighs 500 pounds. The butcher then processes the side of beef, removing 40% of it as waste. He then packages and freezes the rest of the beef for sale in his store. How much did Arlene actually pay for a pound of beef that is ready for sale?

What's the Question?
   a. What is 40% of 500 pounds?
 *b. How much does 1 pound of ready-for-sale beef cost?
   c. How many pounds of waste were there?
   d. How much did Arlene pay for a 500-pound side of beef?
(Answer: Arlene paid approximately $2.08 per pound.)

3. John is preparing for a barbecue for 24 girls on his Little League soft-ball team. He wants to prepare 2 hot dogs for each girl. Hot dogs are packaged 8 to a pack, while buns come in packs of 12. For each hot dog, John must have a bun. Find how many packages of buns John must buy in order for each hot dog to go with a bun.

What's the Question?
   a. How many hot dogs does John need?
   b. How many buns does John need?
   c. How many packages of hot dogs should John buy?
 *d. How many packages of buns should John buy?
(Answer: John should buy 4 packages of buns to get 48 buns.)

4. A pretzel factory produces 12,000 soft pretzels each day. Last Monday, the inspector rejected 15% of the pretzels. The accepted pretzels were then packaged, 30 to a box, for shipping. How many boxes were filled on Monday?

What's the Question?
   a. How many pretzels were rejected on Monday?
   b. How many pretzels were accepted on Monday?
 *c. How many boxes were packed on Monday?
   d. How many pretzels does the factory produce in one day?
(Answer: 340 boxes of pretzels were packed.)

WHAT ARE THE NECESSARY FACTS?

Once the students have successfully identified the question being asked, they must now return to the problem and examine the facts. That is, they must determine which facts are necessary, which facts are extra, and what facts, if any, are missing. This is an important reasoning skill to develop, since, in real-life problems, there usually are more facts than necessary. In some cases, there is insufficient data to successfully resolve the problem. Children must learn to use their critical thinking skills to analyze a problem and to select only those facts that are needed.

In the following pages, we have included forced-choice questions to help students pick out the necessary facts in a problem. In each problem, one or more of the important facts have been omitted, while other extraneous information may appear. The child must select from the given set those facts that are necessary for solving the problem. These exercises differ from the traditional forced-choice questions where only one statement is selected from the given choices. In these questions, one or even all of the choices may be needed. In kindergarten, the teacher should create simple questions similar to these and discuss them orally with the children. Again, we feel that by the time students reach grades 7 and 8, this activity is no longer needed, but should be done orally in class discussion.

We want to reemphasize that once the discussion of the selection of pertinent facts has taken place, it is important to have your students solve each problem.

GRADE 1   (Reproduction Pages 16 and 17)

1. Helen and Alex brought their pet goldfish to school. Helen brought 6 fish. How many fish did Alex bring?

   What's Necessary?
   *a. Together they brought 11 fish.
   b. Alex had fewer fish than Helen.
   (Answer: Alex brought 5 fish to school.)

2. Cookies usually cost 30¢ each. This week, they are on sale. How much do you save when cookies are on sale?

   What's Necessary?
   a. Jordan has 25¢ to spend.
   *b. Cookies cost 20¢ each on sale.
   (Answer: You save 10¢.)

3. The first-grade class is having a picnic. Each car has 4 children and a driver. How many children went to the picnic?

   What's Necessary?
   *a. Five cars were used to take the children to the picnic.
   b. There are 8 adults at the picnic.
   (Answer: 20 children went to the picnic.)

4. Kate has 8 plants. She gave some to her teacher. How many does she have left?

   What's Necessary?
   a. Kate's teacher now has 15 plants.
   b. Michael gave 3 plants to his teacher.
   *c. Kate gave 3 plants to her teacher.
   (Answer: Kate has 5 plants left.)

GRADE 2   (Reproduction Pages 18 and 19)

1. Mrs. Luz is putting on a class play with 10 parts. She already has filled some of the parts. How many more children does she need?

   What's Necessary?
   *a. She already has chosen 7 children for the play.
   b. Fifteen children tried out for the play.
   (Answer: She needs 3 more children.)

2. This past summer, Bernie read 5 more books than Cindy did. How many books did Cindy read?

What's Necessary?
a. Cindy read 3 biographies.
*b. Together they read 15 books.
(Answer: Cindy read 5 books.)

3. Lawrence wants to arrive at school 5 minutes early. School starts at 8:30. At what time should Lawrence leave his house?

What's Necessary?
a. Lawrence's classroom is on the fourth floor.
b. Lawrence takes 20 minutes to eat his breakfast.
*c. It takes Lawrence 20 minutes to walk to school.
(Answer: If it takes him 20 minutes to walk to school, Lawrence should leave at 8:05.)

4. Emily had 90¢. She bought a newspaper and a ball. How much money does she have left?

What's Necessary?
*a. A newspaper costs 25¢.
b. Emily gets 50¢ a week for her allowance.
*c. A ball costs 15¢.
(Answer: She has 50¢ left.)

GRADE 3   (Reproduction Pages 20 and 21)

1. Anita went into the candy store on Thursday. She bought some pretzels. Comic books cost 95¢ each and pretzels cost 20¢ each. How many pretzels did she buy?

What's Necessary?
*a. Anita spent 60¢.
b. Anita has 3 dimes.
c. Candy bars cost 25¢ each.
(Answer: She bought 3 pretzels.)

2. At the cafeteria, Samantha bought a tuna sandwich, a portion of French fries, and a soft drink. How much did she spend?

What's Necessary?
*a. French fries cost 85¢ a portion.
b. Pizza costs $1.55 a slice.
*c. Tuna sandwiches cost $1.25.
*d. Soft drinks cost 95¢ each.
(Answer: She spent $3.05.)

3. Barry gave one of his fish tanks to his sister, Eleanor. Now Eleanor has the same number of tanks as Barry, and she has 16 fish. How many tanks does Eleanor have now?

What's Necessary?
a. Barry now has 12 neon tetras.
*b. Barry started with 5 fish tanks.

c. Eleanor now has 16 neon tetras.
(Answer: She now has 4 tanks.)

4. The ends of a rope are tied to 2 trees. Every 10 feet, a 5-foot post is set into the ground to support the rope. How many support posts are needed?

What's Necessary?
*a. The trees are 100 feet apart.
 b. Each post is 5 feet tall.
 c. The posts are set 2 feet into the ground.
(Answer: 9 posts are needed.)

GRADE 4   (Reproduction Pages 22 and 23)

1. The Nut Shop sells bags of almonds, peanuts, and honey-covered pecans. How many bags of peanuts can Chi buy for the cost of 1 bag of pecans?

What's Necessary?
 a. Almonds cost $1.80 a bag.
*b. Peanuts cost 60¢ a bag.
 c. Walnuts cost $1.00 a bag.
*d. Honey-covered pecans cost $2.40 a bag.
(Answer: One bag of pecans costs $2.40; Chi can buy 4 bags of peanuts.)

2. Ron and his family went to see the doubleheader at the ballpark. The first game lasted exactly 2 hours and 30 minutes. During the intermission between games, Ron had a hot dog and a cold drink. The second game ended at 6:15 P.M. At what time did the second game start?

What's Necessary?
*a. The first game started at 1:00 P.M.
 b. Hot dogs and cold drinks cost $3.00 each.
*c. The intermission between games lasted 30 minutes.
 d. They left home for the stadium at 12:00.
(Answer: The second game started at 4:00.)

3. Ian received a birthday gift from his grandparents. He bought a collection of model racing cars at a local garage sale. He gave 1/3 of them to his sister, Amanda. He gave 1/4 of them to his cousin, Sarah. He gave some of them to his cousin, Emily. He kept the rest for himself. How many cars did he keep?

What's Necessary?
 a. He paid $4.00 for each model car.
*b. He gave 1/6 of them to Emily.
*c. There were 60 cars in the collection.
 d. The gift was a check for $300.
(Answer: He gave 20 cars to Amanda, 15 to Sarah, and 10 to Emily. He kept 15.)

4. There were three rafts floating down the Snake River. In the first raft, the passengers had a total weight of 1,400 pounds. In the second raft, there were 11 people. In the third raft, the average person weighed 159 pounds. Which raft was carrying the most weight?

   What's Necessary?
   *a. The average weight of the people in the second raft was 145 pounds.
   b. There were 10 people in the first raft.
   c. The average weight of the people in the first raft was 140 pounds.
   *d. There were 10 people in the third raft.
   (Answer: Raft 2. Raft 1 = 1,400 pounds; Raft 2 = 1,595 pounds; Raft 3 = 1,590 pounds.)

GRADE 5   (Reproduction Pages 24 and 25)

1. Liu and Tran each bought a pair of running shoes at the local pro shop. How much did each of them spend on their shoes?

   What's Necessary?
   a. Liu had $60.
   b. Tran had $50.
   *c. Liu spent $19 more than Tran on his shoes.
   *d. Together they spent $65 on their shoes.
   (Answer: Tran spent $23; Liu spent $42.)

2. Peter and Paul each entered a Walk-a-Thon to raise money for the children's hospital. Peter had 10 people pledge for his walk, while Paul had 15 people pledge for his. How much money did Peter raise?

   What's Necessary?
   *a. Peter walked 12 miles
   b. Each person pledged $1.00 per mile for Paul.
   *c. Each person pledged $1.25 per mile for Peter.
   d. Paul walked 10 miles.
   (Answer: Peter raised 12 miles × 15 people × $1.25 = $150.)

3. The Junior High School basketball season has just come to an end. Each team played the same number of games. How many more games did the Colts win than the Dragons?

   What's Necessary?
   *a. Each team played 24 games.
   *b. The Colts won 3/4 of their games.
   c. The Cardinals won 2/3 of their games.
   *d. The Dragons won 1/3 of their games.
   (Answer: The Colts won 10 more games than the Dragons.)

4. At the circus, the side show is in a hexagonal tent with a perimeter of 100 yards. There are posts evenly spaced around the perimeter, supporting the tent. On top of each post is a banner. How many banners are used?

What's Necessary?
   a. The circus had 25 banners available.
  *b. The posts are 25 feet apart.
   c. The posts are placed 5 feet deep into the ground.
   d. The tent has 6 sides.
   (Answer: 12 posts are needed.)

GRADE 6   (Reproduction Pages 26 and 27)

1. Mr. Marshall bought 30 prizes for his math class. The prizes were pins and trophies. How much did he spend for the pins?

    What's Necessary?
    *a. Pins cost $4 each.
     b. Trophies cost $8 each.
    *c. He bought twice as many pins as trophies.
     (Answer: He bought 20 pins at $4 each and spent $80.)

2. Sandee is at the sale at a local stereo store. She bought CDs and audio-tapes. How much money does she have left?

    What's Necessary?
     a. She bought 6 audiotapes.
    *b. She spent $13 for audiotapes.
     c. She bought 4 CDs.
    *d. She spent $25 for CDs.
    *e. She started with $50.
     (Answer: Sandee has $12 left.)

3. Workers are setting up the seats for the fall concert. One-half of the seats are in the blue section. One-fourth of the seats are in the red section. One-eighth of the seats are in the green section. The rest are in the balcony. If all seats are sold, the concert will take in $320. How many seats are in the red section?

    What's Necessary?
     a. Blue section seats cost $9.00 each.
    *b. There are 5 seats in the balcony.
     c. Red section seats cost $8.00 each.
     d. There are twice as many seats in the blue section as in the red.
     (Answer: There are 40 seats in all; 10 are in the red section.)

4. Mike, David, Jeff, Danny, and Jerry were driving golf balls at the local driving range. How far did Danny drive the ball?

    What's Necessary?
     a. Mike missed the ball completely.
     b. David's drive went 4 yards farther than Jerry's.
    *c. Jeff's drive went 220 yards.
     d. Jeff's drive was 2 yards shorter than Jerry's.
    *e. Danny's drive went 4 yards beyond Jeff's.
     (Answer: Danny's drive went 224 yards.)

CHAPTER FOUR

Formulated Response Questions

The formulated response question requires that the student "formulate" his or her own response to a given problem. In other words, a problem is presented to the student and he or she must construct a solution and indicate the answer. *There must also be an explanation of the solution.* This explanation can range from a drawing, an equation, or just a few words, all the way to a complete paragraph. This extended response on the part of the student permits the teacher to analyze the student's reasoning and problem-solving ability. This question is often referred to as a *performance task.* It allows students to demonstrate their abilities to collect, organize, describe, display, and interpret data in a meaningful situation.

How does the performance task differ from the traditional "word problems" that teachers have put on tests for years? Basically, it doesn't! However, with the current emphasis on problem solving and reasoning, the performance task question should not be one that has been discussed nor dwelled upon in class. Rather, it should be a "problem" as opposed to a "review exercise." In addition, the major difference lies in the requirement of an explanatory statement or paragraph.

Formulated response questions are scored in a traditional manner, with partial credit being given when the student demonstrates the proper direction, and full credit only when the solution and the answer are both correct *and* when the explanatory statement is consistent with the solution. This is the place where the analytic rubric comes into play. For each performance task, decide in advance what will constitute achievement in each of the four categories: "Understands the problem," "Selects a plan," "Carries out the plan," and "Communicates the solution" (see Reproduction Page 5). Be certain that the students know that a written explanation must accompany their solutions. We have found that a discussion of the generic analytic rubric with the students is an excellent teaching device.

In each of the tasks that follow, we will present a problem, a solution (or solutions), and "specific assessment characteristics—what to look for" section. In the problems designed for the primary grades, the specific assessment characteristics may take the form of oral questions to be asked and/or responses to look for. These might deal particularly with understanding the problem, as well as the direction taken by the children in their attempts to resolve the situation. Use these specific assessment characteristics together with the generic analytic rubric in your assessment of these performance tasks.

PERFORMANCE TASKS

GRADES K–2   Due to the limited facility in reading and writing in these early grades, the assessment techniques that you can use here are pretty much restricted to observations and discussions. In many cases, the tasks will be in picture form and you will have to present them verbally to the children. While the children can work on these tasks individually, we suggest that the solutions be attempted by small groups or even the entire class working collectively.

PROBLEM 1   (Reproduction Page 28)
Anna wants to have the same number of fish in each tank. What should she do? How many fish will be in each tank?

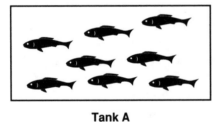   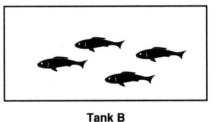

Tank A   **Tank B**

Solution   Take 2 fish from the first tank and put them into the other tank. This puts 6 fish in each tank.

Specific Assessment Characteristics—What to Look For
1. What are we trying to do?
2. Did the children use counters to simulate the fish?
3. Did they move 1 counter at a time from tank A to tank B until the tanks each had the same number?
    OR
4. Did they put all the counters together into one pile and then distribute them into two equal piles?
    OR
5. Did they do the problem mentally?
6. Did they end up with 6 fish in each tank?

PROBLEM 2   (Reproduction Page 29)
Mrs. Edmunds brought 6 plants to school. Alex has to put them into 3 window boxes. Each window box must have at least 1 plant. How should he do it?

Solution   In this problem, the order of the window boxes is disregarded. This problem also has multiple answers:

    4–1–1,   3–2–1,   2–2–2

Specific Assessment Characteristics—What to Look For
1. Did the children use manipulatives to simulate the plants?
2. Were all 6 plants distributed, and were all 3 window boxes used?
3. Did they arrive at a correct answer?
4. Did the children recognize that there was more than one answer?
5. Did they find all 3 answers?

PROBLEM 3   (Reproduction Page 30)
There are 6 children at Carla's party. Anna and Janet left early. How many children are now at the party?

Solution   6 – 2 = 4. There are now 4 children at the party.

Specific Assessment Characteristics—What to Look For
1. Did the children use manipulatives to simulate the children?
    OR
2. Did they solve the problem mentally?
3. Did they recognize the subtraction concept?
4. Did they obtain the correct answer?

PROBLEM 4   (Reproduction Page 31)
Dick and Jane are sitting on a log in the carrot patch. They see a fox family with 7 foxes. How many ears are there for 7 foxes?

Solution   There are 14 ears:

    Use a table and continue the pattern, or

Use manipulatives and count, or

Skip count by 2s.

Specific Assessment Characteristics—What to Look For
1. Did the children use manipulatives to simulate the story?
2. Did they use a table to simulate the story?
3. Did they associate 2 ears with each fox?
4. Did they arrive at the correct answer?

PROBLEM 5   (Reproduction Page 32)

Are there more monkeys or bears in the zoo? How many more?

Solution   There are more monkeys than bears.

8 − 6 = 2. There are 2 more monkeys.

Specific Assessment Characteristics—What to Look For
1. Did the children find all the monkeys and all the bears in the picture?
2. Did they recognize that the number of giraffes is extraneous?
3. Did they use manipulatives to simulate the animals?
4. Did they recognize the difference concept?
5. Did they answer both questions?
6. Were both answers correct?
7. Did any child find the answer by counting?

PROBLEM 6   (Reproduction Page 33)
The children are bird watching. Lucy saw 5 birds. Sean saw 9 birds. Elliott saw the same number of birds as Lucy and Sean saw together. How many birds did Elliot see?

Solution   9 + 5 = 14. Elliot saw 14 birds.

Specific Assessment Characteristics—What to Look For
1. Did the children associate 5 with Lucy and 9 with Sean?

2. Did they use manipulatives to represent the birds?
    OR
3. Did they use tally marks or numerals?
4. Did they recognize that the answer is found by adding how many birds Lucy saw to how many birds Sean saw?
5. Did they get the correct answer?

PROBLEM 7   (Reproduction Page 34)
Nicholas had 3 cookies. He gave 1 to his baby brother, Todd. Then his mother gave Nicholas 2 more cookies. How many cookies does Nicholas have now?

Solution   The solution involves two steps:

$$3 - 1 = 2$$
$$2 + 2 = 4$$

Nicholas now has 4 cookies.

Specific Assessment Characteristics—What to Look For
1. Did the children use manipulatives?
2. Did they use the following plan:
    a. Put 3 counters in a pile.
    b. Remove 1 counter.
    c. Add 2 counters.
    d. Find the total number of counters now in the pile.
3. Did they get the correct answer of 4 ?

PROBLEM 8   (Reproduction Page 35)
On what dates of a month is the sum of the digits equal to 4 ?

Solution   4, 13, 22, 31
        (*Note*: The date *31* is correct only in January, March, May, July, August, October, and December.)

Specific Assessment Characteristics—What to Look For
1. Did the children use a calendar as a resource?
2. Did they make a list of those dates where the digit sum is 4?
3. Did they show that some months do *not* have 31 days?
4. Did they list all 4 (or 3) possible answers?

PROBLEM 9   (Reproduction Page 36)
The children are planting rose bushes in the school yard. They have 16 rose bushes altogether. They decide to put 5 bushes in each row. How many bushes are left over?

Solution   5 + 5 + 5 + 1. There is 1 rose bush left over.

Specific Assessment Characteristics—What to Look For
1. Did the children use counters to represent the rose bushes?
2. Did they put the counters into rows or groups of 5?
3. Did they end up with 1 counter left over?
4. Did they get the correct answer of 1 ?

PROBLEM 10

(Reproduction Page 37)
The children are planting 12 pansies. They want the same number of plants in each row. How should they do this?

Solution

There will be either 5 or 6 answers, depending on whether you will accept 1 row of 12 (with primary-grade children, this is not critical):

12 rows of 1, 6 rows of 2, 4 rows of 3, 3 rows of 4, 2 rows of 6, or 1 row of 12.

Specific Assessment Characteristics—What to Look For
1. Did the children start with 12 counters?
2. Did they partition the set of 12 counters into equal sets?
3. Did they recognize that there was more than one way to arrange the counters?
4. Did they list all 5 (or 6) answers?

PROBLEM 11

(Reproduction Page 38)
It's Halloween! Mrs. Ramirez has a basket of apples. She gives apples to 3 groups of Trick-or-Treaters. The first group got 4 apples. The next group got 3 apples. The next group got 2 apples. Mrs. Ramirez now has 1 apple left. How many apples did she start with?

Solution

$4 + 3 + 2 + 1 = 10$. She started with 10 apples.

Specific Assessment Characteristics—What to Look For
1. Did the children use manipulatives or tallies to simulate the giving away of the apples?
2. Did they remember to include the one apple Mrs. Ramirez had left?
3. Did they recognize that the "3 groups" was extraneous?
4. Did they arrive at 10 as their answer?

PROBLEM 12

(Reproduction Page 39)
Mrs. Rabbit and her 3 baby rabbits each eat 1 carrot a day. How many carrots would the family eat in 1 week?

Solution

$4 + 4 + 4 + 4 + 4 + 4 + 4 = 28$. They eat 28 carrots in a week.

Specific Assessment Characteristics—What to Look For
1. Did the children use manipulatives or tallies to simulate the story?
2. Did they include Mrs. Rabbit as well as her 3 children?
3. Did they add correctly to get 28? Do they know 7 days = 1 week?
4. *Creative solution.* Did any children recognize that $7 \times 4 = 28$?

PROBLEM 13   (Reproduction Page 40)
Maria had 8 postcards to mail from camp. She sent 1 to her mother, 1 to her father, 1 to her sister, and 2 to her friend, Tina. How many did she have left?

Solution $1 + 1 + 1 + 2 = 5$ $8 - 5 = 3$
    OR
$8 - 1 - 1 - 1 - 2 = 3$
    Maria had 3 postcards left.

Specific Assessment Characteristics—What to Look For
1. Did the students simulate the action with a drawing or with counters?
2. Did they recognize subtraction?
3. Did they obtain 3 as their final answer?

PROBLEM 14   (Reproduction Page 41)
Mr. Smith has a jar of jellybeans on his desk. How many jellybeans are in the jar?
1. The number is less than 30.
2. You say the number if you count by 5s.
3. The number is more than 10.
4. You say the number if you count by 4s.

Solution   5 10 15 20 25 and 4 8 12 16 20 24 28. The answer is 20.

Specific Assessment Characteristics—What to Look For
1. Did the children make a list to satisfy the clues?
2. Did they use each successive clue to eliminate specific elements?
3. Did the students arrive at the correct answer of 20?

PROBLEM 15   (Reproduction Page 42)
Milton is standing in line, waiting to get into the movies. There are 5 people in front of him and 3 people in back of him. How many people are standing in line?

Solution $5 + 3 + 1 = 9$. There are 9 people in line.

Specific Assessment Characteristics —What to Look For
1. Did the children make a drawing of the line?
    OR
2. Did they use manipulatives to represent the situation?
3. Did they remember to include Milton?
4. Did they get the correct answer of 9 people?

PROBLEM 16   (Reproduction Page 43)
Reid and Raymond picked up a total of 20 cans from the playground. However, for every 2 cans Reid picked up, Raymond picked up 3. How many cans did each boy pick up?

	Reid	Raymond	Total
Solution	2	3	5
	4	6	10
	6	9	15
	8	12	20

Reid picked up 8 cans and Raymond picked up 12 cans.
   OR
Start with 20 counters. Remove 2 and 3 at each juncture. Put them into separate piles until all the counters are gone.

Specific Assessment Characteristics—What to Look For
1. Did the children simulate the action with a table or counters?
2. Did they recognize that each action consisted of 2 parts? (When Reid gets 2, Raymond gets 3.)
3. Did they use all of the counters?
4. Did they add the number in each set?
5. Did they get both answers correct ?

PROBLEM 17   (Reproduction Page 44)
Ann, Barbara, and Carol each have one coin: a nickel, a dime, or a quarter. Barbara's coin is worth the most. Ann's coin is worth more than Carol's. Which coin does each girl have?

	5¢	10¢	25¢
Solution	—	—	Barbara
	Carol	Ann	—
	Carol	Ann	Barbara

Carol has the nickel, Ann has the dime, and Barbara has the quarter.

Specific Assessment Characteristics—What to Look For
1. Did the children use 3 coins or counters to show the action?
2. Did they realize that Barbara has the quarter?
3. Since Ann's coin is worth more than Carol's, did they give the dime to Ann?
4. Did they arrive at all three answers?

PROBLEM 18   (Reproduction Page 45)
Jan is making a necklace with paper shapes. She uses a pattern: 2 red circles, then 1 blue square, then 1 yellow triangle. Then she repeats the pattern. When she finished the necklace, she had used 5 blue squares. How many of each shape did she use?

	Blue Squares	Yellow Triangles	Red Circles
Solution	1	1	2
	1	1	2
	1	1	2
	1	1	2
	1	1	2
	5	5	10

Jan used 5 squares, 5 triangles, and 10 circles.

Specific Assessment Characteristics—What to Look For
1. Did the children make a necklace or simulate with paper and pencil or manipulatives?
2. Did they recognize that the colors were extraneous?
3. Did they recognize that each pattern group contained 2 circles for every 1 square and triangle?
4. Did any child recognize that the pattern consisted of 5 sets?
5. Did they obtain all three answers correctly?

PROBLEM 19

(Reproduction Page 46)
You are making rock turtles. You need 1 large rock for the body and 5 small rocks for the head and legs. You have 10 large rocks and 25 small rocks. How many rock turtles can you make?

Solution

There are 5 sets of legs and heads available. There are 10 "bodies" available. Only 5 rock turtles can be made. (There will be 5 large rocks left over.)

Specific Assessment Characteristics—What to Look For
1. Did the children assemble 10 large counters and 25 small counters?
2. Did they build turtles using 5 small and 1 large counter for each?
3. Did they build exactly 5 complete turtles?
4. Did they recognize that there is an excess number of bodies and that the total number depends only on the small "rocks"—that is, how many 5s are there in 25?

PROBLEM 20

(Reproduction Page 47)
Mr. Elroy and his 3 helpers each make 1 duck decoy per day. How many do they make in a week?

Solution

3 + 1 = 4 people

4 × 7 days = 28 decoys

(Some children may question whether Mr. Elroy and his helpers would work a 7-day week. This should be discussed.)

Specific Assessment Characteristics—What to Look For
1. Did the children recognize that there were 4 people making the decoys?

2. Did they make 7 sets of 4 objects each?
3. Did they arrive at 28 duck decoys?

PROBLEM 21   (Reproduction Page 48)
The In-and-Out Sandwich Shop has 5 different sandwiches on its menu: tuna, turkey, hamburger, hot dog, and chicken salad. The Milou family ate at the Sandwich Shop twice last week. Mr. Milou ordered a tuna sandwich and a hot dog. Mrs. Milou ordered a hamburger both times. Eric had one turkey sandwich and one chicken salad sandwich. Mimi had a tuna sandwich and a hot dog. Maggie had a hamburger and a chicken salad sandwich. Which kind of sandwich was ordered most by the family?

Solution

	Tuna	Turkey	Hamburger	Hot Dog	Chicken Salad
Mr. Milou	1			1	
Mrs. Milou			2		
Eric		1			1
Mimi	1			1	
Maggie			1		1
Totals	2	1	3	2	2

The hamburger was ordered most.

Specific Assessment Characteristics—What to Look For
1. Did the children make a table or a list?
    OR
2. Did they use a mat and tokens?
3. Did they make tally marks to represent the sandwiches?
    OR
4. Did they put tokens in each box on the mat?
5. Did they arrive at the hamburger as the most often ordered sandwich?

PROBLEM 22   (Reproduction Page 49)
The gum ball machine in Mr. Waldo's store has gum balls that are red, green, or yellow. Each gum ball costs 25¢. How many quarters do you need to be certain that you have 2 gum balls of the same color?

Solution   At worst, you could get 1 red, 1 green, and 1 yellow gum ball after the first three trials. The fourth gum ball must yield 2 of the same color. Thus, you need 4 quarters to ensure 2 of one color.

Specific Assessment Characteristics—What to Look For
1. Did the children understand the difference between "*may* get 2 of the same color" versus "*must* get 2 of the same color"?
2. Did they recognize that the first 3 gum balls could be 1 red, 1 green, and 1 yellow, which would make a fourth trial necessary?
3. Did they get 4 quarters as their answer?

PROBLEM 23   (Reproduction Page 50)
Tyler saw a truck, a car, and a bus go across the bridge. The car crossed the bridge after the bus. The truck crossed the bridge before the bus. In what order did the truck, the car, and the bus go across the bridge?

Solution   Make a time line:

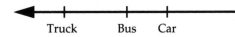

Truck   Bus   Car

Specific Assessment Characteristics—What to Look For
1. Did the children arrange counters or draw a time line to illustrate their understanding of the problem?
2. Are all three vehicles placed on the line?
3. Did the students arrive at the correct order?

PROBLEM 24   (Reproduction Page 51)
Each time the circus juggler appears in the ring, he adds to the number of balls he juggles. The first time he juggles 2 balls. The second time he juggles 4 balls. The third time he juggles 6 balls. If this continues, how many balls will he juggle the fifth time he appears?

Solution   2, 4, 6, 8, 10. He will juggle 10 balls the fifth time.

Specific Assessment Characteristics—What to Look For
1. Did the children illustrate that there is a pattern by skip counting?
    OR
2. Did they use counters to illustrate the pattern?
3. Did they obtain the correct answer?

PROBLEM 25   (Reproduction Page 52)
To earn some extra money in school, Phil buys and sells old comic books. He buys them for 10¢ each and sells them for 15¢ each. How many comic books must he sell to earn 50¢?

Solution   15¢ – 10¢ = 5¢ (profit per book)
50¢ ÷ 5¢ = 10

Phil must sell 10 comic books.

Specific Assessment Characteristics—What to Look For
1. Did the children indicate that there is a 5¢ profit on each comic book Phil sells?
2. Did they understand that the second step involves the division concept? That is, divide the total profit (50¢) by the profit per book (5¢)?
3. Did they get the correct answer of 10 ?

GRADES 3–4

PROBLEM 26   (Reproduction Page 53)
Natalie has 2 quarters and 1 nickel. A candy bar costs 20¢. How many candy bars can Natalie buy?

Solution   She has 55¢.

> 1 candy bar = 20¢
> 2 candy bars = 40¢
> 3 candy bars = 60¢ (Too much!)

She can buy 1 or 2 candy bars.

Specific Assessment Characteristics—What to Look For
1. Did the students show that Natalie has 55¢?
2. Did they show that 3 candy bars will cost more than 55¢?
3. Did they list *both* possible answers?

PROBLEM 27   (Reproduction Page 54)
A fence encloses a garden that is in the shape of a square. Each side has 4 posts. What's the smallest number of posts you need?

Solution   Make a drawing:

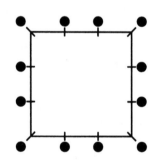

You need 12 posts.

Specific Assessment Characteristics—What to Look For
1. Did the students make a drawing to show the situation?
2. Did they indicate "posts" in each corner?
3. Did they indicate that each corner post counts on two sides?
4. Did they get the correct answer?

PROBLEM 28   (Reproduction Page 55)
In a 3-person tournament, George scored 8 points. Ivan scored twice as many as George. Lynn scored 7 more points than George. Who was the winner and what was his or her score?

Solution   George = 8
Ivan = $2 \times 8 = 16$
Lynn = $8 + 7 = 15$

Ivan was the winner and scored 16 points.

Specific Assessment Characteristics—What to Look For
1. Did the students show each person's score?
2. Did they order the scores correctly?
3. Did they answer the question by stating both the winner (Ivan) and his score (16)?

PROBLEM 29   (Reproduction Page 56)
Maureen saves $1.50 a week to buy a video game. The video game costs $21.00 and she has already saved $6.00. How many more weeks must she save before she can buy the game?

Solution $21.00 − $6.00 = $15.00 (to be saved)
$15.00 ÷ $1.50 = 10

She must save for 10 more weeks.

Specific Assessment Characteristics—What to Look For
1. Did the students subtract $21.00 − $6.00 to find how much more Maureen must save?
2. Did they use division to arrive at the answer?
   OR
3. Did they use repeated subtraction of $1.50 to get the answer?
4. Did they get the correct answer of 10 weeks?

PROBLEM 30   (Reproduction Page 57)
Karl bought 10 tulip bulbs at 2 for $2.00. The bulbs usually cost $1.25 each. How much did Karl pay for the bulbs?

Solution $10 ÷ 2 = 5$
$5 \times $2.00 = 10.00
   OR
2 for $2.00 = $1.00 per bulb
10 bulbs = $10.00

Specific Assessment Characteristics—What to Look For
1. Did the students ignore the $1.25 usual price (extraneous information)?
2. Did they divide by 2 to obtain the number of units of bulbs Karl bought—namely, 5?
   OR
3. Did they find the unit cost?

4. Did they obtain $10.00 as their final answer?

PROBLEM 31   (Reproduction Page 58)
Justin works in the party store, filling helium balloons. Mrs. Adams ordered 70 balloons, some blue and some silver. She wants 20 more silver than blue. How many of each should Justin inflate?

Solution   Use the guess-and-test strategy.

Blue	Silver	
10	30	(Not 70)
20	40	(Not 70)
30	50	(80—Too many)
25	45	Yes!

Justin will inflate 45 silver and 25 blue balloons.
OR

$70 - 20 = 50$

$50 \div 2 = 25$

$25 + 20 = 45$

Justin fills 25 blue and 45 silver.

Specific Assessment Characteristics—What to Look For
1. Did the students show that there are 70 balloons?
2. Did they indicate a difference of 20?
3. If the students used the guess-and-test strategy, did they include an organized table?
4. Did they obtain *both* answers?

PROBLEM 32   (Reproduction Page 59)
Pam and her mother went shopping. She spent $18 on a new blouse and $7 for a hat. She then spent $5 for a scarf and $12 for a new purse. If she had $5 left, how much did Pam start with?

Solution $18 +$7 +$5 + $12 = $42 spent
$42 + $5 (Pam had left) = $47

Pam started with $47.00.

Specific Assessment Characteristics—What to Look For
1. Did the students find the total expenditures of $42?
2. Did they add the $5 Pam had left?
3. Did the students arrive at the correct answer?

PROBLEM 33   (Reproduction Page 60)
Greg has 36 baseball cards. His sister Rhona has 24. How many cards must Greg give to Rhona so that they each have the same number of cards? How many cards will each have?

Solution

36 − 24 = 12 (There is a 12-card difference.)
12 ÷ 2 = 6
36 − 6 = 30 and 24 + 6 = 30

Greg must give Rhona 6 cards. Each person will have 30 cards.

Specific Assessment Characteristics—What to Look For
1. Did the students use two sets of counters (36 and 24) and move them from one pile to the other, until both piles contained the same number of tokens?
   OR
2. Did the students solve the problem using subtraction and division?
3. Did they show that, at the end of the problem, each child has 30 cards ?
4. Did they show both answers?
5. *Creative solution.* Did any student find the total number of cards and divide by 2? (i.e., 36 + 24 = 60; 60 ÷ 2 = 30)

PROBLEM 34   (Reproduction Page 61)
The monorail that rides around the zoo is 84 feet long. It has 4 cars, each 18 feet long. What is the distance between each car, if the distances between the cars is the same?

Solution

4 cars × 18 feet each = 72 feet
84 feet − 72 feet = 12 feet

If there are 4 cars, there are 3 intervals between cars.

12 ÷ 3 = 4

The distance between the cars is 4 feet.

Specific Assessment Characteristics—What to Look For
1. Did the students make a drawing or a sketch?
2. Did the drawing show the dimensions and the intervals?
3. Did they compute the total length of the 4 cars?
4. Did they subtract the length of the 4 cars from the length of the monorail?
5. Did they divide by 3 rather than by 4?
6. Did they get the correct answer?

PROBLEM 35   (Reproduction Page 62)
Simone bought 5 audiotapes from her tape club. The price of each tape is the same, and there is a $3.00 handling charge for the entire order. Her total bill was $23.00. What was the price for each tape?

Solution $23.00 – $3.00 = $20.00 (the price of 5 tapes)

$20.00 ÷ 5 = $4.00

Each tape is priced at $4.00.

Specific Assessment Characteristics—What to Look For
1. Did the students subtract the handling charge?
2. Did they show that the $3.00 charge was for the entire order, not per tape?
3. Did they divide the $20.00 cost by 5?
4. Did they arrive at the correct answer?

PROBLEM 36   (Reproduction Page 63)
At a local amusement park, the "Big Pelican Revue" takes place 4 times each day. The theater has 220 seats. Last Friday, 815 people saw the revue. How many empty seats were there last Friday?

Solution   220 × 4 = 880 seats per day

880 – 815 = 65 empty seats

There were 65 empty seats last Friday.

Specific Assessment Characteristics—What to Look For
1. Did the students find that there were a total of 880 seats available?
2. Did they subtract the 815 occupied seats?
3. Did they arrive at the correct answer of 65 empty seats?

PROBLEM 37   (Reproduction Page 64)
The charge for renting a rowboat is $5.00 per hour for each of the first two hours, and $3.00 for each additional hour or fractional part. Louise and Rose rented a rowboat at 1:00 P.M. and brought it back at 5:30 P.M. How much did it cost them?

Solution   1:00 to 3:00 = 2 hours @ $5.00 = $10.00

3:00 to 5:30 = 2 1/2 hours, but they are charged for 3 hours

3 hours @ $3.00 = $9.00

Total Cost = $10.00 + $9.00 = $19.00

Specific Assessment Characteristics—What to Look For
1. Did the students divide the problem into two parts—namely, 2 hours at $5.00 per hour and the rest at $3.00 per hour?
2. Did they recognize that, for the remaining 2 1/2 hours, Louise and Rose would be charged for 3 hours?
3. Did they compute each charge separately?
4. Did they add the two charges?
5. Did they arrive at the correct answer?

PROBLEM 38   (Reproduction Page 65)

There are 6 children seated around a table in a cooperative learning group. Their names are Alice, Bob, Carol, Dennis, Edward, and Fran. Their teacher, Ms. Chang, has 50 multiple drill cards. She passes them around the table until they are all gone. Alice gets the first card, Bob gets the second card, and so on. Who gets the 50th card?

Solution   One possible solution is to take 50 counters and act out the problem
                    OR
Make a table to simulate the action:

A	B	C	D	E	F
1	2	3	4	5	6
7	8	9	10	11	12
13	14	15	16	17	18
		. . .			
49	50				

The fiftieth card goes to Bob.
    OR
A creative student might recognize that the position of a card depends on the remainder when the number is divided by 6. In other words, if $R = 1$, the card goes to Alice; if $R = 2$, the card goes to Bob; if $R = 3$, the card goes to Carol, and so on. If $R = 0$, the card goes to Fran.

Specific Assessment Characteristics—What to Look For
1. Did the students simulate the action by taking 50 counters and placing them into 6 piles, one at a time?
    OR
2. Did the students make a table assigning the numbers to the appropriate columns?
3. Did they arrive at the correct answer?

PROBLEM 39   (Reproduction Page 66)

The local chess club is holding a "round-robin" tournament with 5 players. Each player plays one match against each of the other players. How many chess matches will be played in the tournament?

Solution   Make a table showing the matches:

A–B
A–C   B–C
A–D   B–D   C–D
A–E   B–E   C–E   D–E

There will be 10 matches in the tournament.

Specific Assessment Characteristics—What to Look For
1. Did the students make a table?

2. Did they recognize that A playing B is the same match as B playing A?
3. Did they include all the matches?
4. Did they arrive at 10 matches for the answer?

PROBLEM 40   (Reproduction Page 67)
Maury is putting his blocks into a set of toy trains. He builds the first three trains as follows:

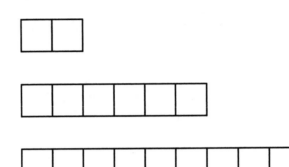

If he continues in this manner, how many blocks will be needed for the sixth train?

Solution   Make a table:

Train Number	1	2	3	4	5	6
Blocks Used	2	6	10	14	18	22

Maury will use 22 blocks on the sixth train.

Specific Assessment Characteristics—What to Look For
1. Did the students write the sequence of numbers 2, 6, 10, . . . ?
2. Did they make a table to organize the data?
3. Did they recognize the pattern that each train contains 4 more blocks than the previous train?
4. Did they carry the sequence out to the sixth term?
5. Did they arrive at the correct answer?

PROBLEM 41   (Reproduction Page 68)
Lauren went to the Water Wonder Amusement Park on Tuesday. She bought tickets for two rides. She gave the ticket seller a $10 bill and received $3.75 in change. What two rides did she buy tickets for?

White Water Raft	$3.50
Hi-Bump	$3.00
Water Slide	$2.75
Tubing Ride	$2.00
Kiddy Shower	$1.00

Solution First, determine how much money Lauren spent:

$10-00 – $3.75 = $6.25 (the amount she spent)

White Water Raft = $3.50

Water Slide   = $2.75

$3.50 + $2.75   = $6.25

She bought tickets for the White Water Raft and the Water Slide.

Specific Assessment Characteristics—What to Look For
1. Did the students determine that Lauren spent $6.25?
2. Did they select as one ride the Water Slide, because the price of one ride must end with a 5?
3. Did they obtain both answers?

PROBLEM 42 (Reproduction Page 69)
Douglas and Seth are both working part time at the local pizza shop. Douglas works 1 day and then has 2 days off. Seth works 1 day and then has 3 days off. If they both work on March 1, on what other days in March will they both work?

Solution Make a table:

	1	2	3	4	5	6	7	8	9	10	11	12	13	14	...	25
Douglas	X	-	-	X	-	-	X	-	-	X	-	-	X	-		X
Seth	X	-	-	-	X	-	-	-	X	-	-	-	X	-	...	X

They work together on March 1, March 13, and March 25.

Specific Assessment Characteristics—What to Look For
1. Did the students make a table/calendar showing 31 days?
2. Did they show Douglas's schedule as March 1, 4, 7, 10, 13, 16, 19,...?
3. Did they show Seth's schedule as March 1, 5, 9, 13, 17,...?
4. Did they arrive at March 1, 13, and 25 as the dates on which they both work?
5. *Creative solution.* Did any student recognize that the answer depends on common multiples of 3 and 4—namely, 12-day intervals?

PROBLEM 43   (Reproduction Page 70)
The faces of a cube are numbered in order. Part of the cube is shown in the figure below. What is the sum of the numbers on the faces of the cube?

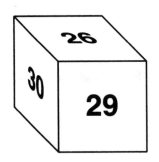

Solution   There are two possible answers:

26 + 27 + 28 + 29 + 30 + 31 = 171
OR
25 + 26 + 27 + 28 + 29 + 30 = 165

The sum is either.

Specific Assessment Characteristics—What to Look For
1. Did the students indicate that there are 6 faces on a cube?
2. Did the students show 6 "blanks" with the 3 given numbers properly placed?
3. Did the students fill in the consecutive blanks with the appropriate set of numbers?
4. Did they get the correct answer (*either* sum)?
5. *Creative solution.* Does any student recognize that there are two possible answers and give both?

PROBLEM 44   (Reproduction Page 71)
Jeff, Amy, Nancy, and Dan have formed a club. The club needs a president and a treasurer. They decide that each month they will change positions until all possible combinations have been used. How many months can they do this before they must repeat?

Solution   Make an organized list of the possible pairings.

P	T	P	T	P	T	P	T
J	A	A	J	D	J	N	J
J	D	A	D	D	A	N	A
J	N	A	N	D	N	N	D

They can continue for 12 months without repeating.

Specific Assessment Characteristics—What to Look For
1. Did the students make an exhaustive list?

2. Did they show that *Jeff (President)–Amy (Treasurer)* is not the same as *Amy(President)–Jeff (Treasurer)* ?
3. Did they list all the possibilities?
4. Did they get the correct answer of 12 months?

PROBLEM 45

(Reproduction Page 72)
Four girls are waiting in line to buy tickets to the ball game. Charlotte is between Dominique and Vicki. Loretta is last in line, next to Dominique. Who is first in line?

Solution

Make a line drawing:

Vicki is first in line.

Specific Assessment Characteristics—What to Look For
1. Did the students show a line drawing?
2. Did they show Loretta as last in the line?
3. Did they show Dominique just in front of Loretta?
4. Did they place Charlotte between Vicki and Dominique?
5. Did they show Vicki as first in line?

PROBLEM 46

(Reproduction Page 73)
Four friends went into a local ice cream parlor. Each ordered a different flavor: vanilla, chocolate, strawberry, and butter pecan. Aaron doesn't like vanilla. Kari's brother ordered vanilla. Kari cannot eat nuts because they stick in her braces. Barry handed the chocolate cone to Dolores and kept the vanilla cone for himself. Who ordered each flavor?

Solution

Prepare a 4 × 4 matrix. Fill in the boxes using the given clues.

	Vanilla	*Chocolate*	*Strawberry*	*Butter Pecan*
Aaron	X	X	X	✓
Barry	✓	X	X	X
Kari	X	X	✓	X
Dolores	X	✓	X	X

Aaron ordered butter pecan, Barry ordered vanilla, Kari ordered strawberry, and Dolores ordered chocolate.

Specific Assessment Characteristics—What to Look For
1. Did the students make a 4 × 4 matrix?
2. Did they label it correctly?
3. Did they use each clue properly?

PROBLEM 47   (Reproduction Page 74)
William and Hillary are shooting darts. William has already scored 17 with his 5 darts. Hillary has shot 4 of hers, and hit the target as shown. What must Hillary score on her final dart to beat William?

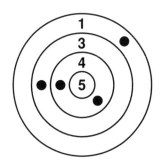

Solution   Hillary has already scored 1 + 3 + 4 + 4, or 12 points. Since the largest number on the target is 5, she can score, at most, 12 + 5, or 17 points. Thus she cannot beat William.

Specific Assessment Characteristics—What to Look For
1. Did the students add Hillary's four scores to get 12?
2. Did they indicate that to beat William, Hillary must score at least 6 points?
3. Did they show Hillary's maximum score as 17?
4. Did they answer correctly that Hillary cannot beat William?

PROBLEM 48   (Reproduction Page 75)
A firefighter is standing on the middle rung of a ladder. He moved up 7 rungs on the ladder, but the smoke got too heavy, so he stepped down 11 rungs. When the smoke finally cleared, he went up the 17 remaining rungs to the top of the ladder. How many rungs are on the ladder?

Solution   Simulate with a drawing and arrows, or:

+7 –11 + 17 = 13 rungs above the middle

13 + 13 = 26 rungs (not including the middle one)

There are 27 rungs on the ladder.

Specific Assessment Characteristics—What to Look For
1. Did the students simulate the action with a series of directed arrows or with a series of adding and subtracting numbers?
2. Did they begin on the middle rung of the ladder?

3. Did they remember to add the 13 rungs above and below the middle rung?
4. Did they include the middle rung?
5. Did they arrive at 27 rungs as their answer?

PROBLEM 49   (Reproduction Page 76)
Aleksi brought a bag with 36 oranges home from Florida to give to his neighbors. He gave one neighbor 11 oranges, a second neighbor 9 oranges, and a third neighbor 7 oranges. If he continues giving the oranges away in this manner, how many neighbors will receive oranges?

Solution

Neighbor	Number Given	Total Given
1	11	11
2	9	20
3	7	27
4	5	32
5	3	35
6	1	36

Six neighbors will receive oranges.

Specific Assessment Characteristics—What to Look For
1. Did the students make a table?
2. Did they continue the pattern 11, 9, 7, . . . ?
3. Did they show the number of oranges given each time?
4. Did they include the interim totals after each distribution?
5. Did they give the correct answer of 6 neighbors?

PROBLEM 50   (Reproduction Page 77)
Pablo, Quentin, Ronald, and Steve are in an elimination tennis tournament. Pablo lost to Steve in the first round. Ronald played Steve in the second round. Ronald won one match and lost one match. Who won the tournament?

Solution   Make a tournament tree diagram:

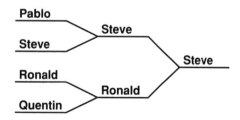

Steve won the tournament.

Specific Assessment Characteristics—What to Look For

1. Did the students make a tree diagram?
2. Did they show the first-round opponents correctly?
3. Did they show that "Ronald played Steve in the second round" means that Ronald must have beaten Quentin in Round 1?
4. Since Ronald won 1 match and lost 1 match, did they show that Steve beat Ronald in the second round to win the tournament?

GRADES 5–6

PROBLEM 51

(Reproduction Page 78)
Tasha buys and sells baseball cards as a hobby. Last month, she bought some rookie cards and paid $3 for every 5 cards. Later, she was offered $3 for every 4 cards. She sold them all and made a profit of $9 on the entire lot. How many rookie cards did she buy and sell?

Solution

The following steps are needed:

$3.00 for every 5 cards = 60¢ per card

$3.00 for every 4 cards = 75¢ per card

Her profit is 75¢ – 60¢ = 15¢ per card.

Total profit = $9.00; 15¢ = .15

$9.00 ÷ .15 = 60

She bought and sold 60 cards.

Specific Assessment Characteristics—What to Look For
1. Did the students determine the cost, 60¢, of each card ?
2. Did they determine the selling price, 75¢, of each card ?
3. Did they determine the profit on each card—namely, 15¢?
4. Did they show the division of $9.00 by 15¢?
5. Did they arrive at the correct answer of 60 cards?
6. *Creative solution.* Did any students show that the number of cards Tasha bought and sold must be a multiple of 5 and 4? Thus, using the guess-and-test strategy, they would try 20, 40, 60 until they arrived at 60 as the answer.

PROBLEM 52

(Reproduction Page 79)
The indoor soccer league started the season with three teams: the Roaches, the Scorpions, and the Tarantulas. Each team played 1 home game and 1 road game against each of the other teams.

   a. The Roaches never beat the Scorpions.
   b. The Tarantulas never lost a home game.
   c. The Tarantulas lost 2 games.

Find the win-and-loss record for each team.

Solution   Make a table:

Home	R	Ⓡ	Ⓢ	Ⓢ	Ⓣ	Ⓣ
Away	Ⓢ	T	R	T	R	S

    Clue (a) tells the Scorpions won 2 games against the Roaches. Put a circle around the Scorpions in those 2 games.

    Clue (b) says the Tarantulas won both home games, so put a circle around the Tarantulas in their 2 home games.

    Clue (c) says the Tarantulas lost 2 games, thus the Roaches and the Scorpions each beat them one time. Put a circle around the Roaches and Scorpions in these games.

    The win-and-loss records were: Roaches   1–3
                                    Scorpions 3–1
                                    Tarantulas 2–2

Specific Assessment Characteristics—What to Look For
1. Did the students organize their work with a table?
2. Did they use each clue to determine the wins and losses?
3. Did they show that a win for a team is also a loss for its opponent?
4. Did they arrive at the *three* correct win-and-loss records?

PROBLEM 53   (Reproduction Page 80)
Lion cubs were born at the local zoo last week. The zookeeper weighed them two at a time, and got weights of 13, 14, and 15 pounds. How many lion cubs were there and what was the weight of each cub to the nearest pound?

Solution   By simulation or guess and test, there are 3 cubs. They are weighed as A-B, A-C, and B-C. Now use guess-and-test:

$$6 + 7 = 13$$
$$6 + 8 = 14$$
$$7 + 8 = 15$$

There were 3 cubs, whose weights were 6 pounds, 7 pounds, and 8 pounds.

Specific Assessment Characteristics—What to Look For

1. Did the students determine that in order to have three weighings, there must have been 3 cubs?
2. Did the students indicate that no two cubs could weigh the same, or there would not have been 3 different sums?
3. Did they use guess-and-test?
4. Did they arrive at the correct weights?

PROBLEM 54   (Reproduction Page 81)
At the drugstore, Sondra can buy one postcard for a nickel, or 6 postcards for a quarter. What is the least it will cost her to buy 21 postcards?

Solution   Use this logic:

> 6 cards = 25¢   6 cards = 25¢
> 6 cards = 25¢   3 cards = 15¢
> 25¢ + 25¢ + 25¢ + 15¢ = 90¢

Specific Assessment Characteristics—What to Look For
1. Did the students show that the best price is obtained by using three groups of 6 and 3 single cards?
2. Did they perform the multiplication and the addition correctly?
3. Did they obtain the correct answer?

PROBLEM 55   (Reproduction Page 82)
Harry and Ezra entered a Walk-a-Thon to raise money for charity. They each had 10 people pledge $1.25 for each mile they walked. Together they earned $250 for the charity. How many miles did they walk altogether?

Solution   There are basically two solutions to the problem. The more obvious one is arrived at by assuming that they both walked the same number of miles.
$1.25 per mile for each mile = $2.50 per mile together for each person who made a pledge. Thus, they earned $25 per mile together.
$250 ÷ $25 = 10 miles each, total 20 miles.
OR
A more interesting case would be if Harry and Ezra did *not* each walk the same number of miles. However, the answer is still 20 miles altogether.
$1.25 per mile for each mile walked = $12.50 for each mile walked (10 people × $1.25)
$250 ÷ $12.50 = 20 miles.
Together they walked 20 miles.

Specific Assessment Characteristics—What to Look For
1. Did the students know that Harry and Ezra each earned $12.50 (10 × $1.25) for each mile walked?
2. Did the students show that the amount earned together for each mile was $25?
3. Did they divide $250 by $25?
4. Did they obtain the correct answer of 20 miles?

PROBLEM 56   (Reproduction Page 83)
Juanita reads at the rate of 20 pages in 30 minutes. She is now on page 235 of a book that ends on page 345. How long will it take her to complete the book?

Solution   There are two ways to solve this problem.

345 − 235 = 110 pages to finish

110 ÷ 20 = 5 + Remainder 10

Thus, Juanita will take

5 × 30 minutes = 150 minutes

+ 10 × 1 1/2 minutes = 15 minutes

A total of 165 minutes, which equals 2 hours and 45 minutes.

OR

20 pages in 30 minutes = 1 1/2 minutes per page

110 pages × 1 1/2 = 165 minutes = 2 hours 45 minutes

Specific Assessment Characteristics—What to Look For
1. Did the students indicate that Juanita must still read 110 pages?
2. Did they use units of 20 pages per 30 minutes?
   OR
3. Did they use 1 1/2 minutes per page?
4. Did they obtain 5 1/2 of the 30-minute units to get 165 minutes?
   OR
5. Did they multiply 1 1/2 × 110 pages to get 165 minutes?
6. Did the students obtain 165 minutes, or 2 hours 45 minutes, as their answer?

PROBLEM 57

(Reproduction Page 84)
The auditorium in the town concert hall is organized by color-coded sections. One-half of the seats are in the blue orchestra section. One-fourth are in the red side section. One-eighth are in the green balcony section. The remaining 5 seats are on the stage side. How many seats are in each section?

Solution

1/2 + 1/4 + 1/8 = 7/8
The remaining 1/8 must represent the 5 remaining seats. There must be 8 × 5 or 40 seats in the auditorium. Of these,

20 are in the blue section

10 are in the red section

5 are in the green section

5 are in the yellow section

Specific Assessment Characteristics—What to Look For
1. Did the students show that the 5 seats in the yellow section represent 1/8 of the total?
2. Did they obtain 40 seats as the total number of seats in the auditorium?
3. Did they show all four answers?

PROBLEM 58   (Reproduction Page 85)
Stacey and Bill have 3 pet dogs: Flaky, Shadow, and Lady. Flaky and Lady together eat 1 1/2 cans of dog food each day, whereas Shadow eats 3/4 of a can each day. If dog food costs $1.30 a can, how much do Stacey and Bill spend on dog food for a 4-week, 28-day period?

Solution   1 1/2 + 3/4 = 2 1/4 cans per day
28 days × 2 1/4 = 63 cans
63 × $1.30 = $81.90

They spend $81.90 in a 4-week period.
(Note: The students may use decimal fractions instead of common fractions.)

Specific Assessment Characteristics—What to Look For
1. Do the students demonstrate their understanding by showing appropriate arithmetic procedures?
2. Do they solve the problem in 3 separate stages—that is, (a) the number of cans of dog food eaten each day, (b) the number of cans eaten in 28 days, and (c) the cost for the 28 days?
3. Do they show Lady and Flaky eat 1 1/2 cans together?
4. Do they get the correct answer of $81.90?

PROBLEM 59   (Reproduction Page 86)
The Road Clearing Company is preparing a mixture of salt and sand to be spread on the roads this winter after ice storms. For every pound of salt, there are 3 pounds of sand. The truck holds a total of 2,000 pounds of the mixture. How much salt is in the truckload?

Solution

Salt	Sand	Total
10	30	40
100	300	400
1,000	3,000	4,000
500	1,500	2,000

There will be 500 pounds of salt.
    OR
There are 500 4-pound units in 2,000 pounds. Thus, there will be 500 pounds of salt and 1,500 pounds of sand in these 500 units.

Specific Assessment Characteristics—What to Look For
1. Did the students indicate by drawing or table that for every 4 pounds of mixture, 1 pound is salt and 3 pounds are sand?
2. Did they carry out the table?
    OR
3. Did they divide 2,000 by (units of) 4?
4. Did they obtain the correct answer?

PROBLEM 60   (Reproduction Page 87)
On a softball team, a "battery" consists of a pitcher and a catcher. The local team has 6 pitchers and 2 catchers. How many different batteries can the manager put on the field?

Solution

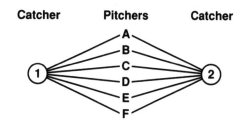

There are 12 possible combinations.
        OR
If the student recognizes the fundamental counting principle, then $6 \times 2 = 12$ is sufficient.

Specific Assessment Characteristics—What to Look For
1. Did the students show a diagram to reveal that, for each catcher, there will be 6 pitchers?
2. Did they arrive at the correct answer?

PROBLEM 61   (Reproduction Page 88)
Melanie is paid by the digit when she uses her calligraphy skills to number the pages in a memory book. There are 99 pages to be numbered. How many times will Melanie write the digit 7?

Solution   Make a list or a table:

Pages	1–9	10–19	20–29	30–39	40–49	50–59	60–69	70–79	80–89	90–99
Number	1	1	1	1	1	1	1	11	1	1

OR

7, 17, 27, 37, 47, 57, 67, 70, 71, 72, 73, 74, 75, 76, 77, 78, 79, 87, 97

There are 20 7s.

Specific Assessment Characteristics—What to Look For
1. Did the students write out all the numbers or make an interval table?
2. Did the students recognize that 77 has two 7s in it?
3. Did they obtain 20 as their answer?

PROBLEM 62   (Reproduction Page 89)
Alex, Helen, and Martha are giving a surprise party for their friend, Mai. They decide to share the expenses equally. Alex spent $35 for a gift, Helen spent $26 for the food, and Martha spent $20 for the decorations. What should they do for each to have spent the same amount?

Solution   Follow these steps:

$35 + $26 + $20 = $81

Each person should contribute $81 ÷ 3 or $27.

Since Martha only spent $20, she must give $7 to Alex. Similarly, Helen should give $1 to Alex.

Specific Assessment Characteristics—What to Look For
1. Did the students show that, for each child to spend the same amount of money, means finding the average amount spent?
2. Did they indicate that each child should have spent $27?
3. Did they indicate that only Alex will receive money—namely, a total of $8?
4. Did they obtain the correct answers?

PROBLEM 63   (Reproduction Page 90)
Mr. Reynolds bought 8 gerbils to give to the two kindergarten classes. How many different ways can he distribute the gerbils to the two classes?

Solution   Make a table:

Class A	7	6	5	4	3	2	1
Class B	1	2	3	4	5	6	7

There are seven different ways to distribute the gerbils.

Specific Assessment Characteristics—What to Look For
1. Did the students show that the total number of gerbils is always 8 ?
2. Did the students show all the possibilities?
3. Did the students recognize that giving 6 to Class A and 2 to Class B is different from giving 6 to Class B and 2 to Class A?
4. Did they show seven different ways?

PROBLEM 64   (Reproduction Page 91)
Mrs. Lyons bought some prizes for her students. She spent $88 altogether on books and audio cassettes. Each book costs $7.00, and each cassette costs $4.00. She bought the same number of each. How many books did she buy?

Solution   One book and one cassette cost $11.00.

88 ÷ 11 = 8 sets (a set consists of 1 book and 1 cassette)

Mrs. Lyons bought 8 books.

Specific Assessment Characteristics—What to Look For
1. Did the students recognize that the prizes were bought in pairs—namely, one of each?
2. Did they show that each pair cost $11.00?
3. Did they divide to obtain 8 sets?
4. Did they get the correct answer of 8 books?
    OR
5. Did the students use the guess-and-test strategy with a table to arrive at the correct answer?

PROBLEM 65

(Reproduction Page 92)
During the family reunion, some members of the Hoffman family decided to go to the zoo. There were more children than adults in the group. They paid $90 for admission. The zoo charges $9 for children and $12 for adults. How many children and how many adults were in the group?

Solution

Use guess-and-test with a table:

Number of Children	× $9.00	Number of Adults	× $12.00	= Total Cost
10	$90	0	0	$90
8	$72	—	$18	—
6	$54	3	$36	$90
2	$18	6	$72	$90

Since there must be more children than adults, only one answer is possible. There were 6 children and 3 adults.

Specific Assessment Characteristics—What to Look For
1. Did the students multiply the number of children × $9.00 and the number of adults × $12.00?
2. Did they add these to obtain $90.00?
3. Did they make a correct table?
4. Did the students recognize that, even though 2 children and 6 adults result in an admission charge of $90.00, there must be more children than adults, so this answer is rejected?
5. Did they arrive at the correct answer of 6 children and 3 adults?

PROBLEM 66

(Reproduction Page 93)
Workers in a store use the same legs to assemble 3-legged stools and 4-legged chairs. Last week, they used 34 legs. How many of each did they make, if they assembled more stools than chairs?

Solution

	Stools:		Chairs:		
	Number × 3 legs		Number × 4 legs		Total Legs
	10	30	1	4	34
	9	27	—	—	—
	8	24	—	—	—
	7	21	—	—	—
	6	18	4	16	34
	5	15	—	—	—
	4	12	—	—	—
	3	9	—	—	—
	2	6	7	28	34

There are three possible answers. However, since they made more stools than chairs, there are two correct answers: 6 stools and 4 chairs, or 10 stools and 1 chair.

Specific Assessment Characteristics—What to Look For
1. Did the students multiply the number of stools by 3 and the number of chairs by 4?
2. Did they show that the total number of legs must be 34?
3. Did they make a table and use the guess-and-test strategy?
4. Did they obtain all three possible answers?
5. Did they arrive at the two correct answers of 6 stools and 4 chairs, as well as 10 stools and 1 chair?

PROBLEM 67

(Reproduction Page 94)
Two boys are paddling a canoe. They leave the dock at 9:00 A.M. and paddle downstream at 6 miles per hour until 11:30 A.M. Then they turn around and paddle upstream at 4 miles per hour until 2:00 P.M. Where are they in relationship to the dock?

Solution

Follow this procedure:

11:30 – 9:00 = 2 1/2 hours

2 1/2 × 6 = 15 miles downstream from the dock

2:00 – 11: 30 = 2 1/2 hours

2 1/2 × 4 = 10 miles back upstream

15 – 10 = 5

The boys are 5 miles downstream from the dock.

Specific Assessment Characteristics—What to Look For
1. Did the students draw a line diagram to show the action?
2. Did they use the rate, time, and distance relationship?
3. Did they find the time (2 1/2 hours) downstream?
4. Did they find the correct distance (15 miles) downstream?
5. Did they find the time (2 1/2 hours) upstream?
6. Did they find the correct distance (10 miles) upstream?

7. Did they find the 5-mile difference?
8. Did they arrive at the correct answer?

PROBLEM 68   (Reproduction Page 95)
The Pizza Shop sells two different sizes of pizza. A regular pizza that is 10 inches in diameter costs $6. A large pizza is 14 inches in diameter and costs $10. Which is the better buy?

Solution   Two separate calculations must be performed:

Regular Pizza

$\pi r^2 = 25\pi = 78.54$ square inches
$\$6.00 \div 78.54 = 8¢$ per square inch (approximately)

Large Pizza

$\pi r^2 = 49\pi = 154$ square inches
$\$10.00 \div 154 = 6¢$ per square inch (approximately)

The large pizza is the better buy.

Specific Assessment Characteristics—What to Look For
1. Did the students calculate the area of each pizza?
2. Did they find the cost per square inch (unit cost) for each pizza?
3. Did they arrive at the correct answer?

PROBLEM 69   (Reproduction Page 96)
A pet store has just received its monthly order. It received 40 more goldfish than ferrets. It received 60 birds. It got 10 fewer canaries than goldfish. It received 20 parakeets. How many pets did the store receive in all?

Solution   Follow this sequence:

The store received 60 birds, of which 20 are parakeets: $60 - 20 = 40$ canaries

This means there were $40 + 10$, or 50, goldfish.

There were $50 - 40$, or 10, ferrets.

The total number of pets was $20 + 40 + 50 + 10 = 120$ pets.

Specific Assessment Characteristics—What to Look For
1. Did the students find the number of canaries using the number of birds?
2. Did they find the number of goldfish as 10 more than the number of canaries?
3. Did they find the number of ferrets as 40 less than the 50 canaries?
4. Did they obtain 120 pets as the answer?

PROBLEM 70

(Reproduction Page 97)
The agricultural school garden is rectangular in shape and measures 20' × 45'. The students plant beans in 2/3 of the garden. One half of that contains lima beans. How many square feet of the garden are planted in lima beans?

Solution

To find the number of square feet:

Area of the garden = 45' × 20' = 900 square feet

Beans = 2/3 × 900 sq ft = 600 square feet

Lima beans = 1/2 × 600 sq ft = 300 square feet

There are 300 square feet planted with lima beans.

Specific Assessment Characteristics—What to Look For
1. Did the students show a rectangle with 45' × 20' dimensions?
2. Did they divide the rectangle into thirds along the 45' dimension?
3. Did they indicate 2/3 of the rectangle or 600 square feet planted in beans?
4. Did they take 1/2 of the 600 square feet for lima beans ?
5. Did they obtain 300 square feet as the answer?
    OR
6. *Creative solution.* Did any student simply take 1/2 × 2/3 × 45 × 20?

PROBLEM 71

(Reproduction Page 98)
Mr. Larson challenged his sixth-grade class to find how many different ways the students could make change for a 50¢ piece, without using pennies. How many different ways were there?

Solution

Make a table:

Q	D	N
0	0	10
0	1	8
0	2	6
0	3	4
0	4	2
0	5	0
1	0	5
1	1	3
1	2	1
2	0	0

There are 10 ways to make change.

Specific Assessment Characteristics—What to Look For
1. Did the students indicate that a quarter = 25¢, a dime = 10¢, and a nickel = 5¢?
2. Did they make a table?
3. Did they show all 10 possible ways to make change?

PROBLEM 72   (Reproduction Page 99)
At the comic book show, Ursula is putting up her display. On the top shelf, she puts 1 *Superman* comic book that she sells for $10.00. On the second shelf, she puts 3 *Batman* comic books that sell for $5.00 each. On the third shelf, she puts 6 *Captain America* comic books. On the fourth shelf, she puts 10 *Spiderman* comic books. If she continues in this way, how many comic books will be in the seven-shelf display?

Solution   Make a table:

Shelf	Number	Total
1	1	1
2	3	4
3	6	10
4	10	20
5	15	35
6	21	56
7	28	84

There will be 84 comic books in Ursula's display.

Specific Assessment Characteristics—What to Look For
1. Did the students show that there are 7 shelves?
2. Did they recognize that the prices were extraneous information?
3. Did they make a table?
4. Did they use the correct pattern: 1, 3, 6, 10, 15, 21, 28?
5. Did they find the *sum* of the comic books on the 7 shelves?
6. Did they arrive at the answer of 84 comic books?

PROBLEM 73   (Reproduction Page 100)
A candy bar is cut into equal pieces. Brittany eats 1/4 of the pieces. Then Nicole eats 1/2 of what is left. Finally, Anthony eats the last 6 pieces. Into how many pieces was the candy bar originally divided?

Solution   The steps to solving this problem are:
Brittany ate 1/4 of the pieces, leaving 3/4.

Nicole ate 1/2 of that 3/4, or 3/8. This leaves 3/4 – 3/8 = 3/8.

Anthony ate eats 6 pieces, which was the 3/8 remaining.

Thus, 6 = 3/8 of the pieces

2 = 1/8 of the pieces

16 = the number of pieces in the entire candy bar (8/8 of the bar)

The candy bar was originally divided into 16 pieces.

Specific Assessment Characteristics—What to Look For
1. Did the students show that Brittany ate 1/4, leaving 3/4 of the candy bar?
2. Did they show that Nicole ate 1/2 of the 3/4 that was left?
3. Did they obtain 3/8 as the last part, the 6 pieces that Anthony ate?
4. Did they get the correct answer of 16 pieces?

PROBLEM 74

(Reproduction Page 101)

Roger spent one-half of his savings to buy a skateboard. Then he spent $12.50 for knee pads and the remaining $25.00 for a helmet. How much did he pay for the skateboard?

Solution

To determine the answer:

$12.50 + $25.00 = $37.50 (which is one-half of Roger's savings—the skateboard is the "other" half).

His skateboard cost $37.50.
    OR
For those students who have had some algebra:

If x represents his savings, then $x/2$ = the cost of the skateboard.

$x/2 + \$12.50 + \$25.00 = x$

$\$37.50 = x/2$

$\$75.00 = x$

His skateboard cost 1/2($75.00) = $37.50.

Specific Assessment Characteristics—What to Look For
1. Did the students show that the cost of the skateboard plus the $12.50 plus the $25.00 is what Roger spent?
2. Did they indicate that the skateboard represents 1/2 of what he spent, or as much as the other two items together?
3. Did they obtain $37.50 as the answer, and not $75.00?

PROBLEM 75

(Reproduction Page 102)

Ron has a rectangle with a perimeter of 30 inches. He divides it into 2 congruent squares. What were the dimensions of the original rectangle?

Solution

Make a drawing:

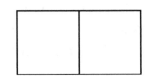

The perimeter of the resulting figure consists of 6 congruent segments, each represented by x:

$$6x = 30$$
$$x = 5$$

The original dimensions were 5" × 10".
    OR
Use guess-and-test with a diagram.

Specific Assessment Characteristics—What to Look For
1. Did the students make a drawing showing the rectangle divided into two congruent squares?
2. Did they show that all 6 segments are congruent?
3. Did they divide by 6?
4. Did they obtain the original dimensions as 5" × 10"?

GRADES 7–8

PROBLEM 76   (Reproduction Page 103)
The roustabouts are setting up a circular pen for the coming rodeo. The fence consists of a set of posts and two 8-foot cross-rails between each pair of posts. The company ordered 40 cross-rails. How many posts will they need?

Solution   Using 40 cross-rails means 20 sections. The total of 20 sections means 20 intervals and 20 posts.

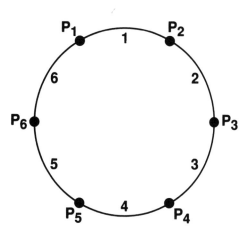

Specific Assessment Characteristics—What to Look For
1. Did the students recognize that the 8-foot length is extraneous?
2. Did the students show that the 40 cross-rails only yields 20 sections?
3. Did they draw a circle to show that the number of arcs is the same as the number of posts? (If it were not a closed figure, an extra end-post would be required.)
4. Did they obtain the correct answer of 20 posts?

PROBLEM 77   (Reproduction Page 104)
David and Claire played a game in which the loser pays the winner 5¢ each time. When they had finished playing, David had won 4 games, but Claire had 20¢ more than when she started. How many games did they play?

Solution

David	W W W W	L L L L	L L L L
Claire	L L L L	W W W W	W W W W

      (David wins)   (Claire wins)   (Claire wins 20¢)

Even

They played 12 games.

Specific Assessment Characteristics—What to Look For
1. Did the students indicate that each game is worth 5¢?
2. Did they show that a win by David means a loss by Claire?
3. Did they show that David won *exactly* 4 games?
4. Did they use a table to simulate the action?
5. Did they indicate that Claire had to win 4 games just to get even?
6. Did they show that Claire had to win 4 more games to win 20¢?
7. Did they obtain the correct answer of 12 games?
8. *Creative solution.* Did they reason that Claire winning 20¢ means she won 4 more games than David? Thus, since David won 4 games, she won 8 games, and they played 12 games in all.

PROBLEM 78   (Reproduction Page 105)
One hexagon has a perimeter of 6 inches. Two hexagons placed side by side have a perimeter of 10 inches. Three hexagons placed side by side have a perimeter of 14 inches. (See the figure below.) What is the perimeter of 8 hexagons placed side by side in a similar fashion?

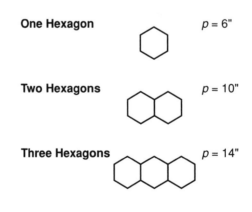

One Hexagon $p = 6"$

Two Hexagons $p = 10"$

Three Hexagons $p = 14"$

Solution   Look for a pattern:

Number of Hexagons	1	2	3	4	5	...	8
Perimeter	6	10	14	18	22	...	34

The perimeter will be 24 inches.

Students may recognize that the perimeter consists of 4 sides for each hexagon, plus the 2 end sides. This translates into the formula:

$$P = 4n + 2$$

where *n* is the number of hexagons.

Specific Assessment Characteristics—What to Look For
1. Did the students draw 8 hexagons and count the perimeter?
   OR
2. Did the students draw a 4-hexagon figure?
   OR
3. Did the students create a table?
4. Did they recognize that the common difference was 4?
5. Did they obtain the correct answer?

PROBLEM 79

(Reproduction Page 106)
Lou has collected 150 insects for his science project. He has exactly one-half of what he needs. Colleen is giving him 15 additional insects. How many does he still have to collect?

Solution

Since Lou has 150 insects, and that is 1/2 of what he needs, he needs 300 insects. Colleen is giving him 15 additional ones.

$$150 + 15 = 165$$
$$300 - 165 = 135$$

Lou needs 135 additional insects.

Specific Assessment Characteristics—What to Look For
1. Did the students show that Lou needs 300 insects altogether?
2. Did they add Colleen's 15 insects to Lou's 150?
3. Did they subtract 165 from 300?
4. Did they obtain the correct answer?

PROBLEM 80

(Reproduction Page 107)
Ray answered 20 questions on his social studies test. He received 5 points for each correct answer, but 2 points were taken off for each incorrect answer. Ray received 72 on his test. How many questions did he answer correctly?

Solution

For algebra students:

Let x = the number correct

$20 - x$ = the number incorrect

$5(x) - 2(20 - x) = 72$

$5x - 40 + 2x = 72$

$7x = 112$

$x = 16$

Ray had 16 correct.
     OR
For students without algebra, use guess-and-test:

Correct	Incorrect	Score
10	10	30 (too small)
15	5	65 (too small)
18	2	86 (too large)
16	4	72 (correct)

Specific Assessment Characteristics—What to Look For
1. Did the students show that the number wrong plus the number right equals 20?
2. Did the students show a +5 for each correct question and a –2 for each incorrect one?
3. Did they obtain the correct answer of 16?

PROBLEM 81   (Reproduction Page 108)
The Sports Emporium is closing out their stock of fishing lures. They had 48 lures left in stock. On Monday, Timothy marked them down to $5.00 each and sold 1/2 of them. On Tuesday, he marked the remaining lures down to $4.00 each and sold 1/3 of them. On Wednesday, he marked the remaining lures down to $3.00 and sold 1/4 of them. On Thursday, he marked the rest down to $2.00 and sold them all. He had paid $3.00 for each lure. How much money did the store make or lose on the sale?

Solution

	Number Sold	Number Left	Price	Amount
Monday	24	24	$5	$120
Tuesday	8	16	$4	$ 32
Wednesday	4	12	$3	$ 12
Thursday	12	0	$2	$ 24
				$ 188

Cost = 48 lures $\times$ $3.00 = $144

$188 – $144 = $44.00 profit

Specific Assessment Characteristics—What to Look For
1. Did the students calculate the total cost as $144.00?
2. Did they show the number of lures sold each day?
3. Did they compute the amount of money taken in each day?
4. Did they calculate how many were left over at the end of each day?
5. Did they calculate the total income of $188.00?
6. Did the students obtain the correct answer of a profit of $44.00?

PROBLEM 82

(Reproduction Page 109)
The school cafeteria offers a complete lunch for $2.00, consisting of an appetizer, a main dish, and a dessert. All the lunches come with a container of milk. Today, the appetizer is soup or juice. The main dish is a hot dog, a hamburger, or a slice of pizza. For dessert, you can choose pudding or apple pie. How many different lunches could you pick?

Solution

If a student recognizes the fundamental counting principle, then $2 \times 3 \times 2 = 12$ different lunches are possible. Otherwise, make a tree diagram:

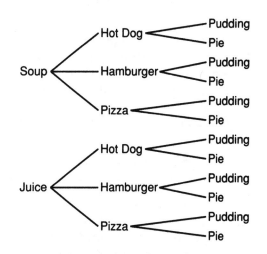

There are 12 possible lunches.

Specific Assessment Characteristics—What to Look For
1. Did the students realize that the container of milk and the $2.00 cost were extraneous information?
2. Did the students multiply $2 \times 3 \times 2$?
   OR
3. Did the students make a tree diagram?
4. Did they pair each main course with each appetizer?
5. Did they pair each appetizer with each dessert?
6. Did they arrive at the correct answer?

PROBLEM 83   (Reproduction Page 110)
When the giant clock in the town hall chimes, each chime takes 1/2 second. There is a 2-second interval between chimes. Thus, when it is 4 o'clock, the chiming takes 8 seconds. At that same rate, how long will it take to chime at 8:00?

Solution

```
/   /   /   /   /   /   /   /
1   2   3   4   5   6   7   8
```

There are 8 chimes and 7 intervals.

$8 \times 1/2 = 4$
$7 \times 2 = 14$

It will take 4 + 14 or 18 seconds to chime at 8:00.

Specific Assessment Characteristics—What to Look For
1. Did the students show that there are 8 chimes but only 7 intervals?
2. Did they calculate the time for 8 chimes as 4 seconds?
3. Did they calculate the time for 7 intervals as 14 seconds?
4. Did they obtain the correct answer of 18 seconds?

PROBLEM 84   (Reproduction Page 111)
Lisa ate 1/2 of the mini-muffins in the refrigerator and her brother Lorenzo ate 1/4 of them. Finally, their mother ate the remaining 6 mini-muffins. How many mini-muffins did Lisa eat?

Solution   Follow these steps:

Lisa ate 1/2, Lorenzo ate 1/4, thus there were 3/4 eaten.

Their mother ate the remaining 1/4 or 6.

Thus, there were 24 mini-muffins in all, and Lisa ate 12.

Specific Assessment Characteristics—What to Look For
1. Did the students add the fractions 1/2 + 1/4 ?
2. Did they subtract that sum from 1, to get the part that their mother ate?
3. Did they get 1/4 = 6 ?
4. Did they obtain 24 as the total number of mini-muffins?
5. Did they obtain 12 as their answer?

PROBLEM 85   (Reproduction Page 112)
Two boys are paddling a canoe. They leave the dock at 9:00 A.M. and paddle downstream at 6 miles per hour. At 10:30 A.M., they turn around and start upstream at the rate of 4 miles per hour. At what time do they return to the dock?

Solution

1 1/2 hours at 6 miles per hour = 9 miles downstream from the dock

9 miles ÷ 4 miles per hour = 2 1/4 hours (time it takes to get back)

10:30 + 2 1/4 hours = 12:45 P.M.

They will arrive back at the dock at 12:45 P.M.

Specific Assessment Characteristics—What to Look For
1. Did the students draw a line diagram to show the action?
2. Did the students show the downstream calculations to obtain a distance of 9 miles from the dock?
3. Did they show that 9 miles is the distance the boys must paddle upstream, in order to return to the dock?
4. Did they use the R × T = D relationship properly to obtain the return time?
5. Did they add the times correctly to obtain 12:45 P.M.?

PROBLEM 86

(Reproduction Page 113)
Mona has $20 less than Jasmine. Laura has $20 less than Mona. Together, all three girls have $87.00. How much does each girl have?

Solution

For students with an algebra background:

Let x = the amount of money Mona has,

then $x + 20$ = the amount of money Jasmine has,

$x - 20$ = the amount of money Laura has.

$$x + 20 + x + x - 20 = 87$$
$$3x = 87$$
$$x = 29$$

Laura has $9.00, Mona has $29.00, and Jasmine has $49.00.

For students without an algebra background, use the guess-and-test strategy.

Specific Assessment Characteristics—What to Look For

For Algebra Students:

1. Did the students express each person's amount of money algebraically in terms of one of them?
2. Did they show that the sum of all their money was $87.00?
3. Did they write an appropriate equation?
4. Did they solve their equation correctly?
5. Did they obtain all three correct answers?

For Nonalgebra Students:

1. Did they use guess-and-test?
2. Did their guesses reflect a total of $87.00?
3. Did each person's amount of money differ by $20.00?
4. Did they obtain all three correct answers?

PROBLEM 87

(Reproduction Page 114)
Mr. and Mrs. Cooper are each starting a new job. Mr. Cooper will start at $30,000 per year and will get a raise of $3,000 per year. Mrs. Cooper will

start at $20,000 but will receive a $5,000 raise per year. When will their salaries be equal?

Solution   Make a table:

Year	Mr. Cooper	Mrs. Cooper
1	$30,000	$20,000
2	$33,000	$25,000
3	$36,000	$30,000
4	$39,000	$35,000
5	$42,000	$40,000
6	$45,000	$45,000

Their salaries will be equal in the sixth year.
    OR
For students who wish to use algebra,

Let x = the number of years it will take until their salaries will be equal :
$$30,000 + 3,000x = 20,000 + 5,000x$$
$$10,000 = 2,000x$$
$$5 = x$$

It will take 5 additional years (after the first), or 6 years, until their salaries are equal.

Specific Assessment Characteristics—What to Look For
1. Did the students make a table to show how much each person earns during each year?
2. Did they begin with the $30,000 and $20,000 salaries?
3. Did they show a $3,000 increase for Mr. Cooper and a $5,000 increase for Mrs. Cooper each year?
4. Did they obtain the correct answer?
    OR
5. Did they write a correct equation to show that the salaries will be equal at some point?
6. Did they solve the equation correctly?
7. Did they realize that the value of the variable, 5, is the number of years it would take for the salaries to be equal, *after the first year*?
8. Did they obtain the correct answer?

PROBLEM 88   (Reproduction Page 115)
Arthur, Pete, and Jacob went into the arcade, each with the same number of tokens. After each of them had used 4 tokens, the total they had left was the same number as each had started with. How many did each person start with?

Solution   Using algebra:

Let x = the number of tokens each boy started with

$3x$ = the total number of tokens they had together

Then, $3x - 12 = x$

$\qquad\qquad 2x = 12$

$\qquad\qquad\; x = 6$

When each boy had used 4 tokens, each had 2 left, or a total of 6. This was the same number each had started with. Each boy started with 6 tokens.

OR

For students without an algebra background, use guess-and-test.

Guess #1

Each started with 10. Then the total is 30. They used 12.

This leaves 18. (Too many.)

Guess #2

Each started with 8. Then the total is 24. They used 12.

This leaves 12. (Still too many.)

Guess #3

Each started with 6. Then the total is 18. They used 12.

This leaves 6. (Correct.)

Each boy started with 6 tokens.

Specific Assessment Characteristics—What to Look For
1. Did the students write a correct equation?
2. Did they show that together the three boys had used 12 tokens?
3. Did they obtain the correct answer, of 6 ?
    OR
4. Did they show that the boys had spent a total of 12 tokens?
5. Did they base each successive guess on the results of the previous one?
6. Did they obtain the correct answer of 6?

PROBLEM 89   (Reproduction Page 116)
There are 210 books on a shelf. There are twice as many mathematics books as history books. There are 10 more science books than mathematics books. How many of each are there?

Solution   Use algebra:

Let x = the number of history books

$2x$ = the number of mathematics books

$2x + 10$ = the number of science books

$$x + 2x + 2x + 10 = 210$$
$$5x + 10 = 210$$
$$5x = 200$$
$$x = 40$$

There are 40 history books, 80 mathematics books, 90 science books.
   OR
Use guess-and-test:

History	Math	Science	Total
50	100	110	260 (too many)
45	90	100	235 (too many)
40	80	90	210 (right!)

There were 40 history books, 80 mathematics books, and 90 science books.

Specific Assessment Characteristics—What to Look For
1. Did the students show that the books on the shelf were history, mathematics, and science?
2. Did they indicate that the history books are the "base" text?
3. Did they set up a proper equation?
       OR
4. Did they solve their equation correctly?
5. Did they use a table with guess-and-test?
6. Did they complete their table?
7. Did they obtain all three correct answers?
8. *Creative solution.* Did any student divide by 10, using 21 books, with only 1 more science book than mathematics book?

PROBLEM 90

(Reproduction Page 117)
A cooking class baked a batch of cookies to sell at the school bake sale. They made between 100 and 150 cookies. One-fourth of the cookies were peanut butter crunch and one-fifth of the cookies were chocolate chip. What is the largest number of cookies the class could have made?

Solution

To solve this problem:

1/4 of the cookies were peanut butter crunch.

1/5 of the cookies were chocolate chip.

The number of cookies the class baked had to be divisible by both 4 and 5, and thus divisible by 20.
   Since the number of cookies was between 100 and 150 and also divisible by 20, the number of cookies had to be either 120 or 140. The greatest number of cookies the class could have baked would be 140.

Specific Assessment Characteristics—What to Look For
1. Did the students show that the number of cookies had to be divisible by both 4 and 5?
2. Did they conclude that the number of cookies had to be divisible by 20?
3. Did they record the possible answers between 100 and 150?
4. Did the students obtain the correct answer?

PROBLEM 91

(Reproduction Page 118)
Georgette is a television repair person. She charges $40 for a service call, which includes up to 1/2 hour of work. She charges $30 for each additional hour or part of an hour. Yesterday, she made 3 calls, lasting 1 hour, 1 3/4 hours, and 2 1/2 hours. How much did she earn yesterday?

Solution

Organize the information with a table:

Call #	Time Spent	Initial Cost	Additional Time	Cost for Extra Time	Total Cost
1	1 hour	$40	1/2 hour	$30	$70
2	1 3/4 hrs	$40	1 1/4 hours	$60	$100
3	2 1/2 hrs	$40	2 hours	$60	$100
					$270

Georgette earned $270.00.

Specific Assessment Characteristics—What to Look For
1. Did the students separate each call into the first 1/2 hour plus additional hours or fractional parts of an hour?
2. Did the students work each call independently?
3. Did the students make a table or use some other appropriate means for organizing the three separate parts of the problem?
4. Did the students show that the initial $40 for each service call included the first 1/2 hour of labor?
5. Did they show that the additional 1/2 hour in call #1 is charged for an entire hour of additional labor?
6. Did they show that the additional 1 1/4 hours in call #2 is charged for 2 hours of additional labor?
7. Did they show that the extra 2 hours in call #3 is charged for 2 hours of additional labor?
8. Did they obtain the correct answer for each of the three parts?
9. Did they obtain the correct answer to the problem?

PROBLEM 92

(Reproduction Page 119)
Brian collects golf balls that fall into the water trap on the golf course, and then sells them as practice balls. He found some golf balls in the morning and arranged them in a square array on his counter. That afternoon, he found 9 more golf balls and discovered that he could now arrange all the

golf balls into a different square array. How many golf balls did he find altogether?

Solution   This problem involves some number theory as well as logic. The two quantities of golf balls are each perfect squares, and differ by 9. List the perfect squares:

   1, 4, 9, 16, 25, 36, 49, 64, 81, . . .

The only two perfect squares that differ by 9 are 16 and 25. Notice that as the squares get larger, the differences increase. Thus Brian found 16 and 9, for a total of 25 golf balls altogether.

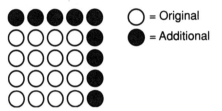

Specific Assessment Characteristics—What to Look For
1. Did the students indicate that the number of golf balls Brian originally found as well as the total number of golf balls were both square numbers?
2. Did the students show that the two square numbers must differ by 9?
3. Did the students make a list of the perfect squares or make a drawing of the possible arrays?
4. Did they obtain the correct answer of 25 golf balls?

PROBLEM 93   (Reproduction Page 120)
The side of an equilateral triangle is 3 inches longer than the side of a square. The perimeter of the square equals the perimeter of the triangle. Find the length of a side of each figure.

Solution   For students with a knowledge of algebra:

   Let s = a side of the square
   $s + 3$ = a side of the equilateral triangle

   Then,

   $4(s) = 3(s + 3)$
   $4s = 3s + 9$
   $s = 9$

A side of the square is 9; a side of the equilateral triangle is 12.
For students without algebra, use guess-and-test.

	Square:		Triangle:	
Side	Perimeter	Side	Perimeter	
1	4	4	12	(no)
2	8	5	15	(no)
3	12	6	18	(no)
.	.	.	.	
.	.	.	.	
.	.	.	.	
9	36	12	36	(yes)

Specific Assessment Characteristics—What to Look For
1. Did the students show that a side of the equilateral triangle is 3 more than a side of the square?
2. If they used algebra, did they write an equation to represent the perimeters?
3. Did they solve the equation correctly?
4. If they used guess-and-test, did they set up an appropriate table?
5. Did they obtain the correct answers?
6. Did they state both answers?

PROBLEM 94

(Reproduction Page 121)
One-Eye Pete left the bank he had just robbed at exactly 1:00 P.M. and headed due south on the trail toward the border at 40 miles per hour. One hour later, the posse started after him on the same trail, traveling at the rate of 60 miles per hour. The border is 100 miles from the bank. Will the posse catch One-Eye before he reaches the border? If yes, how far was One-Eye from escaping? If not, how far from the border was the posse when One-Eye crossed over to safety?

Solution

One-Eye Pete	Posse
D = 100 miles	D = 100 miles
R = 40 miles per hour	R = 60 miles per hour

Since T = D/R, compute the time each takes to reach the border:

T = 2 1/2 hours	T = 1 2/3 hours

One-Eye reaches the border at 3:30 P.M., while the posse reaches the border at 3:40 P.M. One-Eye Pete escaped.

The posse was 10 minutes too late. Since 10 minutes = 1/6 of an hour, $1/6 \times 60 = 10$ miles. The posse was 10 miles from the border when One-Eye Pete escaped.

Specific Assessment Characteristics—What to Look For
1. Did the students calculate the time required by One-Eye Pete to reach the border?
2. Did the students calculate the time required by the posse to reach the border?

3. Did the students realize that the posse left at 2:00 P.M., while One-Eye left at 1:00 P.M.?
4. Did the students answer both questions?
5. Were their answers to both questions correct?

PROBLEM 95   (Reproduction Page 122)
Judy and Marianne made bracelets from beads. They sold some of the bracelets for $1.00, and half as many for $1.50. Altogether, they took in $87.50. How many of each type of bracelet did they make?

Solution   For students who use algebra:

Let x = the number sold at $1.50 each
$2x$ = the number sold at $1.00 each

Then,

$$1.00(2x) + 1.50(x) = 87.50$$
$$2x + 1.5x = 87.50$$
$$3.5x = 87.50$$
$$x = 25$$
$$2x = 50$$

They sold 25 bracelets at $1.50 each and 50 bracelets at $1.00 each.

For students who do not use algebra, use guess-and-test. The number of bracelets sold at $1.00 must be an even number, since the number of bracelets sold for $1.50 each is 1/2 the number of bracelets sold for $1.00 each. Since $87.50 is the amount of money they took in, we can start the guessing with 80.

Number	Income at $1.00	Number	Income at $1.50	TOTAL
80	$80.00	40	$60.00	$140.00 (too much)
60	$60.00	30	$45.00	$105.00 (too much)
40	$40.00	20	$30.00	$70.00 (too little)
50	$50.00	25	$37.50	$87.50 (right)

They sold 50 bracelets at $1.00 each and 25 bracelets at $1.50 each.

Specific Assessment Characteristics—What to Look For
1. Did the students show the two-to-one relationship between the $1.50 bracelets and the $1.00 bracelets?
2. If they used algebra, did they write a correct equation?
3. If they used guess-and-test, did they keep track of their results?
4. Did they obtain both correct answers?

PROBLEM 96   (Reproduction Page 123)
A fuel tank is 3/4 full. When the gauge reads 1/4 full, the owner has the tank completely filled with 600 gallons of fuel. How many gallons does the tank actually hold?

Solution   For those students who use algebra, write an equation or use a proportion:

Equation:

Since the tank was 1/4 full, the 600 gallons represents 3/4 of its capacity. Thus, letting x represent the capacity of the tank,

$$3/4\ (x) = 600$$
$$x = 800$$

The tank has a capacity of 800 gallons.

Proportion:

$$\frac{3}{4} = \frac{600}{x}$$

$$3x = 2400$$
$$x = 800$$

Students who do not use algebra, can reason as follows: Since 3/4 of the tank takes 600 gallons to fill, 1/4 of the tank will equal 200 gallons. Thus the entire tank (4/4) will equal 4 × 200, or 800 gallons.

Specific Assessment Characteristics—What to Look For
1. Did the students realize that the "3/4 full" was extraneous data?
2. Did they show that the 600 gallons was 3/4 of the tank?
3. Did they write an appropriate equation or proportion?
   OR
4. Did they use logic to obtain an answer?
5. Did they obtain the correct answer?

PROBLEM 97   (Reproduction Page 124)
Kim sold 51 jars of her homemade jam in exactly 3 days. Each day she sold 2 more jars than she had sold on the previous day. How many jars of her jam did she sell on each day?

Solution   For students who use algebra:

$$x = \text{the number of jars sold on day 1}$$
$$x + 2 = \text{the number of jars sold on day 2}$$
$$x + 4 = \text{the number of jars sold on day 3}$$

Then,

$$(x) + (x + 2) + (x + 4) = 51$$

$$3x + 6 = 51$$
$$3x = 45$$
$$x = 15$$

Kim sold 15 jars the first day, 17 jars the second day, and 19 jars the third day.

OR

Since she sold 51 jars in 3 days, there must have been an average of 17 jars per day. This represents the number of jars sold on the "middle" day. Since 2 more were sold each day than on the previous day, she sold 15, 17, and 19 jars, respectively.

Specific Assessment Characteristics—What to Look For
1. Did the students recognize that the average number of jars sold was 17?

    OR

2. Did the students write an equation showing that 2 more jars were sold each day after the first day?
3. Did they solve their equation correctly?
4. Did they obtain all three correct answers?

PROBLEM 98   (Reproduction Page 125)
A circular swimming pool is completely surrounded by a walk that is 2 yards wide. The radius of the pool is 50 feet. Find the area of the walk. (Leave your answer in terms of π.)

Solution   Draw a figure to show the situation:

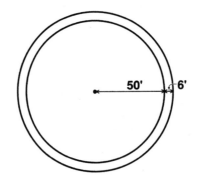

Area of the walk = A (large circle) – A (small circle)
$$A = \pi R^2 - \pi r^2$$

But 2 yards = 6 feet.

$$A = \pi 56^2 - \pi 50^2$$
$$A = 3136\pi - 2500\pi$$
$$A = 636\pi \text{ square feet}$$

Specific Assessment Characteristics—What to Look For
1. Did the students make a drawing of the situation?
2. Did they indicate that the area of the walk was the area of the larger circle minus the area of the smaller circle?
3. Did they change the 2 yards into 6 feet?
4. Did they show the radius of the larger circle to be 50 + 6 = 56 feet?
5. Did they erroneously subtract 56 – 50 *before* squaring?
6. Did they remember to leave their answer in terms of π?
7. Did they obtain the correct answer of 636 π square feet?

PROBLEM 99   (Reproduction Page 126)
A 6" square tray of cornbread can serve four people. How many 12" square trays would be needed to serve 32 people the same amount of cornbread per person?

Solution   Make a drawing:

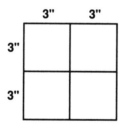

Each serving is 9 square inches.

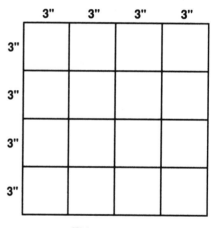

This serves 16.

To serve 32 people, you would need 2 of these trays.

    OR

The area of the 6" square tray = 36 square inches; 36 ÷ 4 = 9 square inches per person.

32 people require 9 × 32 = 288 square inches.

The area of 1 of the 12" trays is 144 square inches.

Thus, we need 2 of these to obtain 288 square inches of cornbread.

Specific Assessment Characteristics—What to Look For
1. Did the students make a drawing to show the size of an individual serving?
    OR

2. Did the students calculate the number of square inches in the original pan and divide by 4 ?
3. Did they calculate the number of square inches of cornbread needed to serve 32 people?
4. Did they obtain the correct answer?

PROBLEM 100   (Reproduction Page 127)
Rachel takes all the marbles from her marble bag and finds that she can arrange the marbles to form a square, containing 13 rows, each of which contains 13 marbles. She finds that she can also arrange them into two smaller squares, with each row of the larger square having 7 more marble than each row of the smaller square. How many marbles are in each row of the two smaller squares?

Solution   For students with a knowledge of algebra,

13 rows × 13 marbles in each row = 169 marbles.

Let n = the number of marbles in the smaller square,

$n + 7$ = the number of marbles in the larger square.

Then,

$$n^2 + (n+7)^2 = 169$$
$$n^2 + n^2 + 14n + 49 = 169$$
$$2n^2 + 14n - 120 = 0$$
$$n^2 + 7n - 60 = 0$$
$$(n+12)(n-5) = 0$$

$$
\begin{array}{c|c}
n + 12 = 0 & n - 5 = 0 \\
n = -12 & n = 5 \\
\text{(Reject)} & n + 7 = 12
\end{array}
$$

The smaller square contains 5 × 5 or 25 marbles; the larger square contains 12 × 12 or 144 marbles.
OR
For students without a knowledge of algebra, use guess-and-test. We want two squares that sum to 169:

1, 4, 9, 16, 25, 36, 49, 64, 81, 100, 121, 144, 169
OR

Guess	Squares	Sum
1, 8	1 + 64	65
2, 9	4 + 81	85
3, 10	9 + 100	109
4, 11	16 + 121	137
5, 12	25 + 144	169

There are 25 and 144 marbles in the 2 smaller squares.

Specific Assessment Characteristics—What to Look For

1. Did the students show that the total number of marbles was 169?
2. Did the students show that the marbles must be divided up into 2 squares whose sum = 169?
3. Did they guess-and-test using integers with a difference of 7?
> OR
4. Did they guess-and-test using the fact that the two squares must total 169?
> OR
5. Did they write a correct equation?
6. Did the students give both correct answers?

CHAPTER FIVE

Projects

In Chapter 2 of this book, we discussed projects as an assessment tool and indicated that we would provide a group of projects that could be assigned in the mathematics class. These projects can be done by individual students or may be assigned to small, cooperative learning groups of three, four, or five students. The projects are not short, one-period assignments; rather, they involve ongoing tasks that may require out-of-class work over a period of a few days to a few weeks to complete. Although the projects are mathematical in nature, they also relate to the real world of the students. This enables the students to understand that mathematics is not something that is confined to their classroom but has real meaning in their everyday lives.

In this chapter, we provide 32 suggestions for projects. In each case, we give a brief description of the project task, together with a connection to one or more other subject areas. (Discussing the project from the point of view of the associated areas is extremely important.) Keep in mind that these are only suggestions. The projects can and should be modified so that they are appropriate for your students. In addition, these projects will suggest others that can be of value to your students. You should develop a file of projects, adding new ones as ideas occur and removing older ones that are no longer useful.

Just as a clear definition of the problem is critical at the beginning of a project task, so, too, is the presentation of the data a critical issue at the end of the investigation. Once the student group has completed its research, the students must decide on the best method for presenting their results. This organizational task involves judgment on the part of the students as to the most appropriate format for presenting their findings to the rest of the class. In fact, a discussion of *why* a particular method of presentation was selected is often a valuable exercise in and of itself.

Projects, like any other reasoning and problem-solving activity, must be assessed. As stated earlier, we recommend the use of the rubric found on Reproduction Page 3 for this purpose.

1. MATHEMATICS/ART (GRADES K–1)

Which color is the favorite in your school or in your class: red, blue, yellow, green, brown, or black?

Teacher's Notes

You may have to work with the entire class to set up the preliminary parts of this activity. Perhaps begin by asking the children to predict which color will be the favorite in their own class. Ask the children how they would expect to find out the results for their own class. Place the six colors on the board or on a large sheet of paper. Have the children come up and make a tally mark or a small check mark right above their own favorite color. Discuss the results of this "pictogram" or "bar graph." Now have the students decide how they can perform this same experiment for specific grades or for the entire school. Perhaps they might wish to compare the results for each grade in the school. Your students might even consider extending this survey to the members of their families, to see if age is a factor.

2. MATHEMATICS/EVERYDAY LIVING (GRADES K–1)

How are the birthdays of the students in your class distributed throughout the year? How many children in your class have birthdays in each month?

Teacher's Notes

Give each child a birthday candle made from poster board or paper. Call out each month of the year in order. Have the children whose birthday occurs in that month come up and put their "candles" into an envelope labeled with that month's name on it. Now have the students count the number of birthday "candles" in each envelope. Prepare a bar graph to show the information. In which month were the fewest birthdays? In which month were the most birthdays? Were there any months with the same number of birthdays? Were there any months in which no pupils have their birthdays?

3. MATHEMATICS/LANGUAGE ARTS (GRADES K–2)

Riddles are fun for younger children. In this project, the students will create a class *Mathematics Riddle Book* of their own.

Teacher's Notes

Ask the students to tell you what a riddle is. What do they think a mathematics riddle is? Give them an example such as: "What has 8 legs, lives on a farm, and gives milk?" (Answer: 2 cows). What has 12 legs, 3 tails, and lives in a pet shop window?" (Answer: 3 rabbits/dogs/cats, etc.). (*Note*: Kindergarten children may have some trouble focusing on the 12 feet and 3 tails at the same time, and may need some further hints from you.)

Divide the class into small groups of four or five students. Have each group write its own riddles about animals, people, or whatever. If the group's riddle is too vague (e.g., "What has 4 legs?"), ask the group to add another clue. The children can also draw pictures to illustrate their riddles.

When the riddles are completed, have each group share some of its work with the rest of the class. Then collect all the finished riddles, duplicate them, and staple them together to form a *Mathematics Riddle Book*. Duplicate enough copies for each student in the class.

4. MATHEMATICS/HEALTH EDUCATION (GRADES 1–2)

Which class in your school has the most missing teeth?

Teacher's Notes

Divide the class into groups of four or five students. Have the children decide how they will find out the information. Will they ask all the students in the school? Or will they make a random sampling of each class? How will they display their results?

5. MATHEMATICS/REAL-WORLD ENVIRONMENT (GRADES 3–4)

What are the amounts of recyclable materials that are thrown away in your home during a typical week, instead of being recycled?

Teacher's Notes

This is a project that can be done in small groups or even with the class as a whole. Students must first determine what are the recyclable materials for which they wish to keep a record. Some recyclable materials might include glass bottles, plastic soda bottles, newspapers, magazines, and so on. An accurate count of each of these items should be kept by each member of the group. Group totals should then be combined and the results presented (perhaps in graphic format) to the entire class.

6. MATHEMATICS/REAL WORLD (GRADES 3–4)

A favorite food today is pizza. What are the most popular toppings in the class? How do the toppings selected by students compare with those selected by their parents?

Teacher's Notes

Divide the class into groups of five students. Help the groups decide which toppings they will investigate. These might include mushrooms, pepperoni, sausage, meatballs, onion, extra cheese, and so forth. Decide how to sample the students and their parents. When the data are collected, the groups should combine their results and then decide how best to present the information to the entire class. Perhaps they might try using a double bar graph.

7. MATHEMATICS/ENGLISH (GRADES 3–4)

How many students' first names must be listed in order to include each letter of the alphabet at least once?

Teacher's Notes

Divide the class into groups of four or five students. Have each group decide on a procedure to follow. Students might begin by listing the names of the students in their own class, one at a time. As they list each name, they can create a frequency table for the letters in the names. How many names did each group list, until all the letters of the alphabet were accounted for?

8. MATHEMATICS/HEALTH EDUCATION (GRADES 3–4)

How many slices of bread does your family eat in three days?

Teacher's Notes

Divide the class into groups of five students. Groups should decide on the procedures they might use to determine the actual number of slices of bread used. One procedure might be to count the number of slices of bread in their houses. (If more bread is purchased during the next three days, add that number of slices to their total.) At the end of the three-day period, count the number of slices of bread left. Now compute how many slices were eaten. Another technique might be to ask family members to record and report the number of slices of bread eaten in the three-day period. Compare results with those of the other groups. Does the number of people in a household affect the amount of bread eaten?

9. MATHEMATICS/ECONOMICS (GRADES 3–4)

Interview three people who work at different jobs. Find out about the world of work.

Teacher's Notes

Divide the class into groups of five students. Have each group decide what questions it will ask. Then devise a questionnaire for the students to use. Include such items as:

What does your job entail? What do you do?

How much preparation do you need to enter the field?

How does mathematics enter into the job you do?

Have all groups prepare a comparison between the jobs they have examined. Discuss each job with the entire class.

10. MATHEMATICS/PHYSICAL EDUCATION (GRADES 5–6)

How many students in your school are left-handed? Is this number consistent throughout each grade?

Teacher's Notes

In the United States, approximately 12 percent of the population is left-handed. Divide your class into groups of four or five students. Each group should discuss the procedures it will follow to solve the problem. Points the children should consider might include: How many students are in each grade? How many students are in the entire school? Will they ask every student or conduct a sample? How will they set up the sampling process? Perhaps each group might work with one grade. How will the data be presented for each grade? For the entire school? Combine the class data. Do they come close to the 12 percent that is the U.S. average? Did all groups obtain the same results? Why or why not?

11. MATHEMATICS/SOCIAL STUDIES (GRADES 5–6)

How many out-of-state license plates will you see in two days? Which states will be the most popular?

Teacher's Notes

Divide the class into groups of four or five students. Have the children decide how and where they will observe the license plates. Will they look in the parking lot of a local mall? Or will they count the out-of-state license on cars as they pass by? Have them keep track of the out-of-state license plates seen in two days. Prepare a list of tallies for their data. Compare the results with the states closest to the one in which the students live. Are the results consistent with the location? Why would they expect this to be so?

12. MATHEMATICS/LANGUAGE ARTS (GRADES 5–6)

Have the students read *Gulliver's Travels*. (Several abridged editions are available for younger students.) Assume that a typical fifth-grade boy in Lilliput is 7 inches tall and weighs 8 1/2 pounds, and a typical Lilliputian girl in the fifth grade is 8 1/2 inches tall and weighs about 9 1/2 pounds. What would the typical classroom in Lilliput look like? Make a scale drawing of the classroom and include a description, drawings, and scale blue prints showing a typical student's desk, a teacher's desk, aisles, chalkboards, pencils, and so on.

In Brobdignag where the people are all giants, a typical fifth-grader might be 16 feet tall and weigh 240 pounds. What would the typical classroom look like in Brobdignag? What might a child's bedroom look like?

Teacher's Notes

In fifth grade, a typical male student is about 55 inches tall and weighs about 68 pounds, while a typical female student is about 65 inches tall and weigh about 78 pounds. Divide the class into groups of four or five. Have the students decide the height and weight of a fifth-grader in their own group. Then use their knowledge of ratio and proportion to complete the project. (The actual linear ratio we have used is 1:8 and the volume unit ratio is 1:512.) The student might actually build a model of a classroom. Have some of the groups work with the Lilliputians (a ratio of 1:8) while the rest work with the Brodbignagians (a ratio of 4:1). Have each group share its blueprints and scale drawings with the rest of the class. Students might conclude their projects by writing a story about what might have happened to them if they visited Lilliput or Brodbignag and had gone to a student's home.

13. MATHEMATICS/EVERYDAY LIVING (GRADES 5–6)

Bananas in a local supermarket recently sold for 59¢ a pound. How much of a pound of bananas is actually eaten? How much is thrown away? How much do bananas actually cost per edible pound?

Teacher's Notes

Divide the class into groups of four or five students. Have each group weigh one banana before peeling. Remove the peel. Now have the group weigh either the unpeeled banana or the peel that has been removed. Do this for several different-sized sample bananas. Count the number of bananas in a "typical" pound. What part of the pound of bananas was wasted? How much do the bananas cost for an edible pound?

Repeat the experiment with peanuts. Now students may have to weigh several peanuts before and after shelling. How many shelled peanuts make one pound?

14. MATHEMATICS/HEALTH EDUCATION (GRADES 5–6)

How much taller is an eighth-grade student than a fifth-grade student?

Teacher's Notes

This activity involves sampling, data collection, and data presentation. The students must make several preliminary decisions as to what constitutes "an eighth-grade student" and "a fifth-grade student." Should they separate boys and girls for this project? How do they find the height of an eighth-grade boy or girl? How can they present their findings to the class? Will the class totals differ from those of the individual groups? Why or why not?

15. MATHEMATICS/DECISION MAKING (GRADES 5–6)

You are going to make a game. The game must have rules and a game board. Be sure to tell how one wins the game.

Teacher's Notes

Students are to create a game. Divide the class into small groups of four or five students. Have them discuss games they like and explain why they like them. Help them develop the parts of games into a series of categories such as materials (dice, coins, spinners, discs, game pieces, etc.), rules of play, the setting of the game, and so on. Each group should develop and write a plan for its game. Include the rules of play, how to win the game, the shape of the board, the equipment needed, and so on. Then have each group make its game. When the group has completed its game, have the students share it with other groups, play the game, and decide whether or not the game is a fair one (each player has an equal chance to win).

16. MATHEMATICS/ECONOMICS (GRADES 5–6)

How much money is spent on postage for the mail your family receives in one week? How many different forms of postage are used? What are they?

Teacher's Notes

Have students estimate the amount of money that they think will be spent on postage for one week. Divide the class into groups. Have each student collect either the actual stamps or a list of the postage used on the mail received at his or her house for one week. Separate the different types of stamps and count the number of each. Have each group make a chart, pictograph, or bar graph showing the number of each type of stamp received during the week. Now combine the results for the entire class. Discuss the impact of "junk mail" on the economy. How close were the students' original estimates of the amount spent on postage to the actual amount?

17. MATHEMATICS/SCIENCE (GRADES 5–6)

The Marvelous Mathematics Manufacturing Company is looking for a new item to manufacture and sell. Your group must design a "book stand," using only free or inexpensive materials, such as paper-towel tubes, cardboard, adhesive tape, scrap cloth, and so forth. Of course, you may also make use of mathematical tools such as rulers, scissors, compasses and the like.

Teacher's Notes

Divide the class into groups of five or six students. Have each group decide exactly what a "book stand" is, then design and build a model of a book stand. Have each group describe its invention, how someone might assemble it, and how to use it. Each group should develop a "catchy" name for its product as well as a radio, television, or newspaper ad campaign for its generic book stand.

18. MATHEMATICS/PHYSICAL EDUCATION (GRADES 5–6)

Select a sport you have never played. Research this sport to find out as much as you can about it. How is mathematics used in this sport?

Teacher's Notes

Students should work in small groups of four or five students. Their research should include such items as a description of the playing field, some of the rules of the sport, equipment they would need and its cost, what kind of uniforms are worn, and so on. Students should look for charts, statistics, scoring records, individual records, and the like. Try to find someone who knows about the sport and interview him or her. Have each group present its sport using a chart, a graph, some data about the sport, and so on. Perhaps the physical education teachers can supply you with a list of some sports that your students are not likely to have played before.

19. MATHEMATICS/SOCIAL STUDIES (GRADES 5–6)

The average new pencil can draw a line that is about 35 miles long. How many pencils would be needed to draw a continuous line around the earth?

Teacher's Notes

Divide the class into groups of four students. Discuss where this line should be drawn. What about over mountains and down through valleys? Over the oceans? Over rivers? Decide on the equator (24,891 miles) as the place to draw the line. Agree to treat the earth as a "flat" surface, and that the pencils can draw a line over anything—water, trees, and so on. The answer turns out to be about 700 pencils.

20. MATHEMATICS/SOCIAL STUDIES (GRADES 7–8)

Traffic lights are supposed to turn red or green at an intersection, depending upon the number of cars that proceed in each direction. Are the traffic lights nearest your school accurately timed?

Teacher's Notes

Use clipboards and stopwatches. Divide the students into groups of five. Two students in each group should time the periods that the light stays red and stays green. Two other students in each group should count the number of cars that proceed through the intersection in both directions. The fifth student records the results. Have students within each group exchange roles and time the number of cars that pass through the other directions when the lights turn green. The students should exchange roles several times and perform the experiment at least three times. Be certain that the experiment is performed at several different times throughout the day. Have the students combine their results and use ratio and proportion to check their work. Discuss the effects that time of day has on the traffic patterns. If the ratios do not appear to be compatible, perhaps the students can write a letter to the Traffic Commissioner in your city to determine why not.

21. MATHEMATICS/SCIENCE (GRADES 7–8)

If you were to "pop" an entire 16-ounce jar of popcorn, how large a container would you need to hold all the popped corn you would have?

Teacher's Notes

This activity involves sampling. Divide the class into groups of four students. Have each group take a sampling. If the container contains 16 ounces of corn to be popped, each group might select 1 ounce. Use different brands of popcorn. Have each group pop the corn (at home or in the home economics room). Measure the size of the container needed to hold that 1 ounce of popped corn. Use ratio and proportion (remember this is a volume discussion) to answer the original question. Discuss why the corn expands when "popped." How much corn would you have to pop to fill your classroom? Why do different brands yield different-sized amounts of popped corn?

22. MATHEMATICS/LANGUAGE ARTS (GRADES 7–8)

What are the most popular (most often used) letters of the alphabet? Suppose you were a contestant on the quiz show *Wheel of Fortune*. Which letters would you guess when it was your turn?

Teacher's Notes

Divide the class into groups of four students. Begin by asking each group to make some predictions. Record the predictions. Then supply each group with a page from the local newspaper. Count the first 100 letters in any article selected at random. Have each group tally its results. Combine the group results. Compare the class results with the original group predictions.

The actual order of frequency for the first 13 letters of the alphabet are:

E T A O N I S R H L D C U

You might ask your students if different newspapers would yield different results. Similarly, would you obtain the same results if you used a magazine such as the *Reader's Digest? The National Enquirer?*

23. MATHEMATICS/SOCIAL STUDIES (GRADES 7–8)

In the United States, there are 49 million dogs and 58 million cats. About 37 percent of all houses have a dog and about 30 percent have a cat. What percent of the houses in your immediate neighborhood have a cat? What percent have a dog? How many have both a cat and a dog?

Teacher's Notes

Divide the class into groups of five students. Have the groups determine how they will perform this experiment. Some groups may decide to have group members survey 100 houses in their neighborhoods. Others may decide to take a sample (perhaps every fifth house?). Each group should decide how it will present its results to the rest of the class. Then combine the data for the entire class. How do these results compare with those for the entire United States? Why is this so? Discuss possible reasons with the class.

24. MATHEMATICS/SOCIAL STUDIES (GRADES 7–8)

Each of the Federal Reserve Banks that issue paper money has a specific letter designation:

A = Boston	E = Richmond	I = Minneapolis
B = New York	F = Atlanta	J = Kansas City
C = Philadelphia	G = Chicago	K = Dallas
D = Cleveland	H = St. Louis	L = San Francisco

Which banks would have the most paper money in circulation near your home?

If you were to look at 10 bills at random, predict how many you think would be from that city.

Teacher's Notes

Discuss with the class where to find the letter designation on a bill. Divide the class into groups of five students. Have each student look at 10 bills chosen at random. List the bank where each was issued along with the denomination of the bill. Combine the data within each group and present the results to the class. Now combine the results for all of the groups and present the data to the class. How close were the original predictions? Why would you expect this to happen? Were all 12 banks represented? Why or why not? Use a large map of the United States. Locate each of the 12 banks on the map. Draw a circle using the bank city as center. Discuss the regions each bank serves. Would you expect some banks to service larger regions? Why?

25. MATHEMATICS/SCIENCE (GRADES 7–8)

Make a model paper airplane. Toss it out of a window in your classroom. Which plane stays in the air the longest time? Why do you think this is so?

Teacher's Notes

Divide the class into groups. Have each group design a model airplane built from paper. Have some members of the class wait outside and signal when each airplane touches the ground. Using stopwatches, time each group's plane. Discuss what factors should be considered to keep the airplane aloft the longest. Permit each group to modify its original design if the group wishes. Conduct the contest again. Then discuss the results with the entire class.

26. MATHEMATICS/HOME ECONOMICS (GRADES 7–8)

How long would it take you to eat an amount of food equal to your own weight?

Teacher's Notes

Divide the students into groups of five. Have each student keep a record of the approximate weight of each item of food that he or she eats for three days. Have the groups compute an "average" weight for the group. Determine how long it would take to eat typical foods that equal this weight. Students should answer such questions as: What is the weight of the food an average student eats in a single day? How long would it take the average student to eat an amount equal to his or her weight? Estimate how many pounds of food that student would eat in one month? In one year?

27. MATHEMATICS/ECONOMICS (GRADES 7–8)

Magazine publishers make most of their money by selling advertising space on the pages of their magazines. Usually they sell ads that are a full page, 1/2 page, 1/3 page, 1/4 page, or 1/8 page. Select a popular magazine that you feel has just about the right "balance" between its content and its advertising material. How much of the total space in the magazine has been given over to advertising?

Teacher's Notes

Divide the class into groups of five or six students. Have each group decide on a single magazine to investigate. Each group should divide its magazine into sections and give each person one section to investigate. Mark each page with the fraction that represents the amount of that page devoted to advertising. Combine results for the entire magazine. Prepare a table or chart to report the results. What part of each magazine was given over to advertising?

28. MATHEMATICS/PHYSICAL EDUCATION (GRADES 7–8)

The students in the fifth grade want to design a new playing field for a game of "Catch-It." If you throw the ball outside of the boundaries, you are "out" and get one point. If you cannot catch a fair ball, you also receive one point. The first player to get five points is the loser. You have 200 feet of rope to mark the boundaries of their playing field. Design a playing field for a game of Catch-It between two players. Design a playing field for a game of Catch-It between five players.

Teacher's Notes

Divide the class into groups of four or five students. Have each group decide what the shape of its playing field should be. Have the students prepare a blueprint or scale drawing of the playing field. The members of each group should present their drawing and the rationale for their choice. Perhaps the class can then go outside and try the game with several of the playing fields that have been designed.

29. MATHEMATICS/ECONOMICS/ART (GRADES 7–8)

There is an empty rectangular lot downtown whose dimensions are 120' × 80' . Its owners wish to convert the lot into a parking lot. Your group has been hired to design the parking lot that will allow for a maximum number of cars. What should the lot look like?

Teacher's Notes

Have students work in groups of four or five students to design the parking lot. Each group should determine what measurements are needed and how to obtain them. The average car requires a parking space that is 12' by 6'. Be certain that the students allow sufficient room for people to get in and out of their cars, and room for cars to make turns, and to back into and out of parking spaces. Allow for the entrance and exit onto adjacent streets. Have students present their diagram and explain their work.

30. MATHEMATICS/PHYSICAL EDUCATION (GRADES 7–8)

Do big people have big feet?

Teacher's Notes

Divide the class into groups of five or six students. Have each group decide on a single grade to investigate and determine how much data are needed and how the data will be obtained. Each group might wish to use a "scatter plot " or other graph to present its data. Groups should discuss the possible need for separate graphs for male and female students. Have the class compare and contrast their data. What conclusions do they arrive at? How might the data be used by sneaker manufacturers to predict how many pairs of sneakers of each size they should make?

31. MATHEMATICS/SPORTS (GRADES 7–8)

How many baseballs are used in a major league baseball game? How much do these baseballs cost a team for the season? How much does major league baseball spend on balls for the entire season, not counting the playoffs and the World Series?

Teacher's Notes

Divide the class into groups of four or five students. Have each group decide how it will find this information. The students might look it up at their local library or decide to call the publicity department of a local major league baseball team. During the typical major league game, approximately 72 baseballs are used, and the cost is about $40 per dozen.

Students should be aware of the fact that, although each team plays a total of 162 games in the regular season, each team is the home team for only 81. It is the responsibility of the home team to supply the baseballs.

32. MATHEMATICS/SCIENCE (GRADES 7–8)

How much water does it take to fill a local swimming pool? What does it weigh?

Teacher's Notes

Divide the class into groups of four or five students. Each group should decide which swimming pool it will investigate, and how to find the dimensions and number of gallons it takes to fill the pool. The students should check their science books to find that water weighs 62.4 pounds per cubic foot.

CHAPTER SIX

Bibliography

Krulik, Stephen, & Rudnick, Jesse A. (1993). *Reasoning and problem solving: A handbook for elementary school teachers.* Boston: Allyn and Bacon.

Krulik, Stephen, & Rudnick, Jesse. (1995). *The new sourcebook for teaching reasoning and problem solving in elementary school.* Boston: Allyn and Bacon.

Lesh, Richard A. (Ed.). (1992). *Assessment of authentic performance in school mathematics.* Washington, DC: American Association for the Advancement of Science.

National Assessment of Educational Progress. (1987). *Learning by doing: A manual for teaching and assessing higher order thinking in science and mathematics.* Princeton, NJ: Educational Testing Service.

National Center for Education Statistics. (1994). *Overview of NAEP assessment frameworks.* Washington, DC: U.S. Department of Education.

National Council of Teachers of Mathematics. (1989). *Curriculum and evaluation standards for school mathematics.* Reston, VA: Author.

National Council of Teachers of Mathematics. (1995). *Assessment standards for school mathematics.* Reston, VA: Author.

Stenmark, Jean K. (Ed.). (1992). *Mathematics assessment—Myths, models, good questions, and practical suggestions.* Reston, VA: National Council of Teachers of Mathematics.

Vermont Department of Education. (1991). *Looking beyond the answer: Vermont's mathematics portfolio assessment program.* Montpelier, VT: Author.

Webb, Norman L. (Ed.). (1993). *Assessment in the mathematics classroom (1993 Yearbook of the N.C.T.M.).* Reston, VA: National Council of Teachers of Mathematics.

Wiggins, Grant P. (1993). *Assessing student performance: Exploring the purpose and limits of testing.* San Francisco: Jossey-Bass.

CHAPTER SEVEN

Reproduction Pages

REPRODUCTION PAGE 1

Student's Name _____ Date _____

OBSERVATION ASSESSMENT FORM

0 = Inadequate   1 = Satisfactory   2 = Good   3 = Exemplary

Category	0	1	2	3	Illustrations
Understands the Problem Facts, questions; illustrates by means of manipulatives, drawings, etc.					
Selects a Plan Appropriate strategy; alternative strategy.					
Carries Out the Plan Carries out strategy; arrives at an answer; effectively does work; carefully organized.					
Reflect Checks computation; reasonableness; answers the question; extends the problem.					
Communication Expresses ideas clearly; orally and/ or written; uses appropriate mathematical language; asks appropriate questions.					
Attitude Patience; perseverance; uses time productively; willing to take risk; enjoys problem solving.					

REPRODUCTION PAGE 2

Student's Name _____ Date _____

INTERVIEW ASSESSMENT FORM

0 = Inadequate   1 = Satisfactory   2 = Good   3 = Exemplary

Category	0	1	2	3	Illustrations
Understands the Problem Facts, questions; illustrates by means of manipulatives, drawings, etc.					
Selects a Plan Appropriate strategy; alternative strategy.					
Carries Out the Plan Carries out strategy; arrives at an answer; effectively does work; carefully organized.					
Reflect Checks computation; reasonableness; answers the question; extends the problem.					
Communication Expresses ideas clearly; orally and/ or written; uses appropriate mathematical language; asks appropriate questions.					
Attitude Patience; perseverance; uses time productively; willing to take risk; enjoys problem solving.					

REPRODUCTION PAGE 3

Student's Name _____ Date _____

PROJECT ASSESSMENT FORM

0 = Inadequate   1 = Satisfactory   2 = Good   3 = Exemplary

Category	0	1	2	3	Illustrations
Design Clearly defines the problem; key mathematical ideas apparent; procedures logical; sets reasonable parameters.					
Implementation Data collected carefully; tasks divided reasonably; carried out in logical fashion.					
Presentation Data organized and analyzed; findings presented carefully, logically, via an appropriate method (drawings, graphs, etc.); oral presentation clear; written presentation clear; resolves the problem or situation.					

Student's Name _____ Date _____

HOLISTIC RUBRIC

Problem Number _____   Score: __ __ __ __ __
                                    4   3   2   1   0

Criteria

4 *Excellent*
The student has:
    selected an appropriate strategy; and
    obtained a correct and complete answer; and
    presented a logical explanation.

3 *Good*
The student has:
    selected an appropriate strategy, implemented it correctly, but made a minor computational error; or
    made a minor interpretive error, but obtained a correct answer based on the interpretation.

2 *Minimally Satisfactory*
The student has:
    answered only part of the problem; or
    made a major computational or conceptual error; or
    selected an appropriate strategy, but did not carry it through.

1 *Inadequate*
The student has:
    indicated the correct data, but has done no work; or
    given a correct answer without work.

0 *No attempt*
The student has:
    given no response; or
    given an irrelevant response.

REPRODUCTION PAGE 5

Student's Name _____ Date _____

ANALYTIC RUBRIC

Characteristics	Criteria	Score
Understands the Problem a. Illustrates the problem with a drawing, table, equation, etc. b. Identifies the necessary data or information c. Identifies the question to be answered	3 = a, b, and c 2 = any 2 of a, b, or c 1 = any 1 of a, b, or c 0 = no meaningful responses	
Selects a Plan a. Selects appropriate strategy and initiates implementation b. Selects appropriate strategy with no implementation or initiates implementation of a questionable strategy c. Inappropriate strategy selected and not implemented d. No meaningful plan shown	3 = a only 2 = b only 1 = c only 0 = d	
Carries Out the Plan Implements plan and shows: a. Correct answer with appropriate work b. Appropriate work with minor computational or interpretation error c. Major interpretative or computational error d. No meaningful response	3 = a only 2 = b only 1 = c only 0 = d	
Communicates the Solution a. Gives the correct answer and a complete, logical explanation of how it was achieved, using appropriate mathematical vocabulary b. Work is neatly and carefully presented with the answer labeled c. Tables and/or diagrams are clearly labeled	3 = a, b, and c 2 = any 2 of a, b, or c 1 = any 1 of a, b, or c 0 = no work shown	
Creativity a. Unusual or unique solution given b. More than one solution c. A generalization	1 = a or b or c	

Student's Name _____ Date _____

WHAT'S THE QUESTION?

1. Mrs. Miller wants to give 2 T-shirts to each of her 6 grandchildren. The T-shirts cost $4.00 each. How many T-shirts must she buy?

   What's the Question?
   a. How many grandchildren does Mrs. Miller have?
   b. How many T-shirts will she give each child?
   c. How many T-shirts does she need?
   d. How much did she spend for the T-shirts?

2. There are 3 boys and 4 girls swimming in the lake. There are 6 girls in canoes. There are 4 boys in rowboats. Find the number of children in boats.

   What's the Question?
   a. How many children are swimming?
   b. How many boys are at the lake?
   c. How many girls are in boats?
   d. How many children are in canoes and rowboats?

Student's Name _____ Date _____

WHAT'S THE QUESTION?

1. There are 12 cookies, 10 pies, 8 cakes, and 5 muffins for sale at the school fair. How many muffins and cakes are for sale?

   What's the Question?
   a. How many cookies are for sale?
   b. How many cakes and muffins are for sale?
   c. How many things are for sale?
   d. How many more pies than muffins are for sale?

2. Antonio has 7 baseball cards left. Find how many cards he started with if he gave 2 cards to Julia and 5 cards to Marian.

   What's the Question?
   a. How many baseball cards did Antonio start with?
   b. How many baseball cards did Antonio give to Julia?
   c. How many baseball cards did Antonio give to Marian?
   d. How many baseball cards did Antonio have left?

REPRODUCTION PAGE 8

Student's Name _____ Date _____

WHAT'S THE QUESTION?

1. Amanda and Ian collect toy cars. Ian has 3 more cars than Amanda.
   Together they have 21 cars. How many cars does Amanda have in her
   collection?

   What's the Question?
   a. How many cars does Ian have?
   b. How many more cars has Ian than Amanda?
   c. How many cars must Amanda get to have the same number as Ian?
   d. How many cars does Amanda have altogether?

2. Antoinette and Martin are the teacher assistants in class today. They
   are giving out the crayons in class. They distribute 144 crayons evenly
   among the 24 children in the room. How many crayons did each child
   receive?

   What's the Question?
   a. How many crayons did Antoinette and Martin give out altogether?
   b. How many children were in the room?
   c. How many crayons did Antoinette and Martin receive?
   d. How many crayons was each child given?

Student's Name _____ Date _____

WHAT'S THE QUESTION?

1. Mrs. Carlyle and her scout troop are involved in an environmental project this month. Gwen and her two girlfriends collected aluminum cans for the month, then took them to the recycling center where they received $24, which they divided equally among themselves. How much did each girl get from the recycling center?

   What's the Question?
   a. How much money did the girls receive altogether?
   b. How much money did each of the three girls receive?
   c. How many girls are in Mrs. Carlyle's troop?
   d. How many cans did Gwen and her friends collect?

2. The local grocery store sold apples at 5¢ for 95¢ each. How much do you save when you buy five apples at a time?

   What's the Question?
   a. How much does one apple cost?
   b. How much do five apples cost?
   c. How much do you save if you buy five apples at a time?
   d. How many apples does the store sell?

Student's Name _____ Date _____

WHAT'S THE QUESTION?

1. There are 36 students in Mrs. Johnson's class. She wishes to form teams of 8 students each. Find the number of students left over after all the teams are chosen.

   What's the Question?
   a. How many students are not placed on a team?
   b. How many students are in the class?
   c. How many students will be on each team?
   d. How many teams will there be in the class?

2. The temperature is rising at a constant rate of 3 degrees each hour. In how many hours will the temperature be at 21 degrees if it is now 6 degrees?

   What's the Question?
   a. What is the temperature at the end of 3 hours?
   b. How many hours will it be until the temperature goes up 21 degrees?
   c. How many hours will it be until the temperature reaches 21 degrees?
   d. How many degrees does the temperature change in 1 hour?

Student's Name _____ Date _____

WHAT'S THE QUESTION?

1. During her spring break, Mandy decided to read a historical novel. There were 485 pages in the book. On the first day, she read 162 pages. On the second day, she read 85 pages, and on the next day, she read 160 pages. How many pages remain to be read?

   What's the Question?
   a. How many pages did Mandy read?
   b. How many pages did Mandy read on the first two days?
   c. How many pages are still left to be read after the third day?
   d. How many pages does the novel contain?

2. A case of paper towels contains 24 rolls and costs the dealer $22.80. He sells each roll for $1.25. How much profit does he make on each roll?

   What's the Question?
   a. How much profit does he make on each case?
   b. How much profit does he make on each roll?
   c. How much does each roll cost the dealer?
   d. How much does the dealer pay for a case of towels?

Student's Name _____ Date _____

WHAT'S THE QUESTION?

1. Jenny bought a 36-picture roll of film for $4.00. She then paid $8.80 to have the film processed. What was the cost of each print she kept, if 4 of the pictures were underexposed and she threw them away?

   What's the Question?
   a. What was the cost of the film?
   b. What was the cost of processing the film?
   c. What was the cost of each good picture?
   d. How much did Jenny spend altogether?

2. Mario and Joanne each bought the exact same car. Mario decided to have power seats and a CD player installed as extras. The power seats cost him $480. Find the cost of the CD player if Joanne paid $18,570 for her car, while Mario paid $19,450 for his.

   What's the Question?
   a. How much did Mario pay for his power seats?
   b. How much did Mario pay for his car?
   c. How much more did Mario pay for his car than Joanne paid for hers?
   d. How much did Mario pay for the CD player?

Student's Name _____ Date _____

WHAT'S THE QUESTION?

1. The Garcia family was driving from Boston, Massachusetts, to Richmond, Virginia. It took them 4 hours to drive the 200 miles from Boston to New York, where they stopped for lunch. They then drove from New York to Philadelphia, a distance of 110 miles in 2 hours, and from Philadelphia to Washington, 150 miles, where they stopped for dinner. Then they continued on for the final 100 miles to Richmond. How far had they driven when they stopped for dinner?

   What's the Question?
   a. What was the length of the trip?
   b. How long did the trip take them?
   c. How far had they driven from Boston to Washington?
   d. How far did they drive after dinner?

2. A 16-inch pizza is cut into 8 equal slices. The pizza contains 3,400 calories and costs $12.60. Four friends shared the pizza equally. Find the number of calories in each slice.

   What's the Question?
   a. How many slices did each person eat?
   b. How much did each person pay?
   c. How many calories did each person eat?
   d. How many calories are in each slice of the pizza?

Student's Name _____ Date _____

WHAT'S THE QUESTION?

1. There are 5 players on the defensive line of the Bearcats football team. Their average weight is 274 pounds. Joe Blue weighs 260 pounds, Marcus Saunders weighs 274 pounds, Orin Chennin weighs 289 pounds, and Leonard Rye weighs 281 pounds. Find the weight of the fifth linesman, Darrin McCoy.

   What's the Question?
   a. What is the weight of the heaviest player on the defensive line?
   b. What is the weight of the lightest player on the defensive line?
   c. What is the weight of the fifth player on the defensive line?
   d. What is the average weight of the 5 players on the defensive line?

2. Arlene is buying beef for a local butcher shop. She paid $1.25 a pound for a side of beef that weighs 500 pounds. The butcher then processes the side of beef, removing 40% of it as waste. He then packages and freezes the rest of the beef for sale in his store. How much did Arlene actually pay for a pound of beef that is ready for sale?

   What's the Question?
   a. What is 40% of 500 pounds?
   b. How much does 1 pound of ready-for-sale beef cost?
   c. How many pounds of waste were there?
   d. How much did Arlene pay for a 500-pound side of beef?

REPRODUCTION PAGE 15

Student's Name _____ Date _____

WHAT'S THE QUESTION?

1. John is preparing a barbecue for 24 girls on his Little League softball team. He wants to prepare 2 hot dogs for each girl. Hot dogs are packaged 8 to a pack, while buns come in packs of 12. For each hot dog, John must have a bun. Find how many packages of buns John must buy in order for each hot dog to go with a bun.

   What's the Question?
   a. How many hot dogs does John need?
   b. How many buns does John need?
   c. How many packages of hot dogs should John buy?
   d. How many packages of buns should John buy?

2. A pretzel factory produces 12,000 soft pretzels each day. Last Monday, the inspector rejected 15% of the pretzels. The accepted pretzels were then packaged, 30 to a box, for shipping. How many boxes were filled on Monday?

   What's the Question?
   a. How many pretzels were rejected on Monday?
   b. How many pretzels were accepted on Monday?
   c. How many boxes were packed on Monday?
   d. How many pretzels does the factory produce in one day?

Student's Name _____ Date _____

WHAT'S NECESSARY?

1. Helen and Alex brought their pet goldfish to school. Helen brought 6 fish. How many fish did Alex bring?

   What's Necessary?
   a. Together they brought 11 fish.
   b. Alex had fewer fish that Helen.

2. Cookies usually cost 30¢ each. This week, they are on sale. How much do you save when cookies are on sale?

   What's Necessary?
   a. Jordan had 25¢ to spend.
   b. Cookies cost 20¢ each on sale.

Student's Name _____ Date _____

WHAT'S NECESSARY?

1. The first-grade class is having a picnic. Each car has 4 children and a driver. How many children went to the picnic?

   What's Necessary?
   a. Five cars were used to take the children to the picnic.
   b. There are 8 adults at the picnic.

2. Kate has 8 plants. She gave some to her teacher. How many does she have left?

   What's Necessary?
   a. Kate's teacher now has 15 plants.
   b. Michael gave 3 plants to his teacher.
   c. Kate gave 3 plants to her teacher.

Student's Name _____ Date _____

WHAT'S NECESSARY?

1. Mrs. Luz is putting on a class play with 10 parts. She already has filled some of the parts. How many more children does she need?

   What's Necessary?
   a. She already has chosen 7 children for the play.
   b. Fifteen children tried out for the play.

2. This past summer, Bernie read 5 more books than Cindy did. How many books did Cindy read?

   What's Necessary?
   a. Cindy read 3 biographies
   b. Together they read 15 books.

Student's Name _____ Date _____

WHAT'S NECESSARY?

1. Lawrence wants to arrive at school 5 minutes early. School starts at 8:30. At what time should Lawrence leave his house?

   What's Necessary?
   a. Lawrence's classroom is on the fourth floor.
   b. Lawrence take 20 minutes to eat his breakfast.
   c. It takes Lawrence 20 minutes to walk to school.

2. Emily has 90¢. She bought a newspaper and a ball. How much money does she have left?

   What's Necessary?
   a. A newspaper costs 25¢.
   b. Emily get 50¢ a week for her allowance.
   c. A ball costs 15¢.

Student's Name _____ Date _____

WHAT'S NECESSARY?

1. Anita went into the candy store on Thursday. She bought some pretzels. Comic books cost 95¢ each and pretzels cost 20¢ each. How many pretzels did she buy?

    What's Necessary?
    a. Anita spent 60¢.
    b. Anita has 3 dimes.
    c. Candy bars cost 25¢ each.

2. At the cafeteria, Samantha bought a tuna sandwich, a portion of French fries, and a soft drink. How much did she spend?

    What's Necessary?
    a. French fries cost 85¢ a portion.
    b. Pizza costs $1.55 a slice.
    c. Tuna sandwiches cost $1.25.
    d. Soft drinks cost 95¢ each.

Student's Name _____ Date _____

WHAT'S NECESSARY?

1. Barry gave one of his fish tanks to his sister, Eleanor. Now Eleanor has the same number of tanks as Barry, and she has 16 fish. How many tanks does Eleanor have now?

   What's Necessary?
   a. Barry now has 12 neon tetras.
   b. Barry started with 5 fish tanks.
   c. Eleanor now has 16 neon tetras.

2. The ends of a rope are tied to 2 trees. Every 10 feet, a 5-foot post is set into the ground to support the rope. How many support posts are needed?

   What's Necessary?
   a. The trees are 100 feet apart.
   b. Each post is 5 feet tall.
   c. The posts are set 2 feet into the ground.

Student's Name _____ Date _____

WHAT'S NECESSARY?

1. The Nut Shop sells bags of almonds, peanuts, and honey-covered pecans. How many bags of peanuts can Chi buy for the cost of 1 bag of pecans?

   What's Necessary?
   a. Almonds cost $1.80 a bag.
   b. Peanuts cost 60¢ a bag.
   c. Walnuts cost $1.00 a bag.
   d. Honey-covered pecans cost $2.40 a bag.

2. Ron and his family went to see the doubleheader at the ballpark. The first game lasted exactly 2 hours and 30 minutes. During the intermission between games, Ron had a hot dog and a cold drink. The second game ended at 6:15 P.M. At what time did the second game start?

   What's Necessary?
   a. The first game started at 1:00 P.M.
   b. Hot dogs and cold drinks cost $3.00 each.
   c. The intermission between games lasted 30 minutes.
   d. They left home for the stadium at 12:00.

Student's Name _____ Date _____

WHAT'S NECESSARY?

1. Ian received a birthday gift from his grandparents. He bought a collection of model racing cars at a local garage sale. He gave 1/3 of them to his sister, Amanda. He gave 1/4 of them to his cousin, Sarah. He gave some of them to his cousin, Emily . He kept the rest for himself. How many cars did he keep?

   What's Necessary?
   a. He paid $4.00 for each model car.
   b. He gave 1/6 of them to Emily.
   c. There were 60 cars in the collection.
   d. The gift was a check for $300.

2. There were three rafts floating down the Snake River. In the first raft, the passengers had a total weight of 1,400 pounds. In the second raft, there were 11 people. In the third raft, the average person weighed 159 pounds. Which raft was carrying the most weight?

   What's Necessary?
   a. The average weight of the people in the second raft was 145 pounds.
   b. There were 10 people in the first raft.
   c. The average weight of the people in the first raft was 140 pounds.
   d. There were 10 people in the third raft.

Student's Name _____ Date _____

WHAT'S NECESSARY?

1. Liu and Tran each bought a pair of running shoes at the local pro shop. How much did each of them spend on their shoes?

   What's Necessary?
   a. Liu had $60.
   b. Tran had $50.
   c. Liu spent $19 more than Tran on his shoes.
   d. Together they spent $65 on their shoes.

2. Peter and Paul each entered a Walk-a-Thon to raise money for the children's hospital. Peter had 10 people pledge for his walk, while Paul had 15 people pledge for his. How much money did Peter raise?

   What's Necessary?
   a. Peter walked 12 miles.
   b. Each person pledged $1.00 per mile for Paul.
   c. Each person pledged $1.25 a mile for Peter.
   d. Paul walked 10 miles.

Student's Name _____ Date _____

WHAT'S NECESSARY?

1. The Junior High School basketball season has just come to an end. Each team played the same number of games. How many more games did the Colts win than the Dragons?

   What's Necessary?
   a. Each team played 24 games.
   b. The Colts won 3/4 of their games.
   c. The Cardinals won 2/3 of their games.
   d. The Dragons won 1/3 of their games.

2. At the circus, the side show is in a hexagonal tent with a perimeter of 100 yards. There are posts evenly spaced around the perimeter, supporting the tent. On top of each post is a banner. How many banners are used?

   What's Necessary?
   a. The circus had 25 banners available.
   b. The posts are 25 feet apart.
   c. The posts are placed 5 feet deep into the ground.
   d. The tent has 6 sides.

Student's Name _____ Date _____

WHAT'S NECESSARY?

1. Mr. Marshall bought 30 prizes for his math class. The prizes were pins and trophies. How much did he spend for the pins?

   What's Necessary?
   a. Pins cost $4 each.
   b. Trophies cost $8 each.
   c. He bought twice as many pins as trophies.

2. Sandee is at the sale at a local stereo store. She bought CDs and audio-tapes. How much money does she have left?

   What's Necessary?
   a. She bought 6 audiotapes.
   b. She spent $13 for audiotapes.
   c. She bought 4 CDs.
   d. She spent $25 for CDs.
   e. She started with $50.

Student's Name _____ Date _____

WHAT'S NECESSARY?

1. Workers are setting up the seats for the fall concert. One-half of the seats are in the blue section. One-fourth of the seats are in the red section. One-eighth of the seats are in the green section. The rest are in the balcony. If all seats are sold, the concert will take in $320. How many seats are in the red section?

   What's Necessary?
   a. Blue section seats cost $9.00 each.
   b. There are 5 seats in the balcony.
   c. Red section seats cost $8.00 each.
   d. There are twice as many seats in the blue section as in the red.

2. Mike, David, Jeff, Danny, and Jerry were driving golf balls at the local driving range. How far did Danny drive the ball?

   What's Necessary?
   a. Mike missed the ball completely.
   b. David's drive went 4 yards farther than Jerry's.
   c. Jeff's drive went 220 yards.
   d. Jeff's drive was 2 yards shorter than Jerry's.
   e. Danny's drive went 4 yards beyond Jeff's.

Student's Name _____ Date _____

PROBLEM

Anna wants to have the same number of fish in each tank. What should she do? How many fish will be in each tank?

Tank A   **Tank B**

Student's Name _____ Date _____

PROBLEM

Mrs. Edmunds brought 6 plants to school. Alex has to put them into 3 window boxes. Each window box must have at least 1 plant. How should he do it?

Student's Name _____ Date _____

PROBLEM

There are 6 children at Carla's party. Anna and Janet left early. How many children are now at the party?

Student's Name _____ Date _____

PROBLEM

Dick and Jane are sitting on a log in the carrot patch. They see a fox family with 7 foxes. How many ears are there for 7 foxes?

1 Fox   2 Ears

2 Foxes 4 Ears

3 Foxes 6 Ears

Student's Name _____ Date _____

PROBLEM

Are there more monkeys or bears in the zoo? How many more?

Student's Name _____ Date _____

PROBLEM

The children are bird watching. Lucy saw 5 birds. Sean saw 9 birds. Elliott saw the same number of birds as Lucy and Sean saw together. How many birds did Elliott see?

Student's Name _____ Date _____

PROBLEM

Nicholas had 3 cookies. He gave 1 to his baby brother, Todd. Then his mother gave Nicholas 2 more cookies. How many cookies does Nicholas have now?

Student's Name _____ Date _____

PROBLEM

On what dates of a month is the sum of the digits equal to 4?

Student's Name _____ Date _____

PROBLEM

The children are planting rose bushes in the school yard. They have 16 rose bushes altogether. They decide to put 5 bushes in each row. How many bushes are left over?

Student's Name _____ Date _____

PROBLEM

The children are planting 12 pansies. They want the same number of plants in each row. How should they do this?

Student's Name _____ Date _____

PROBLEM

It's Halloween! Mrs. Ramirez has a basket of apples. She gives apples to 3 groups of Trick-or-Treaters. The first group got 4 apples. The next group got 3 apples. The next group got 2 apples. Mrs. Ramirez now has 1 apple left. How many apples did she start with?

Student's Name _____ Date _____

PROBLEM

Mrs. Rabbit and her 3 baby rabbits each eat 1 carrot a day. How many carrots would the family eat in 1 week?

REPRODUCTION PAGE 40

Student's Name _____ Date _____

PROBLEM

Maria had 8 postcards to mail from camp. She sent 1 to her mother, 1 to her father, 1 to her sister, and 2 to her friend, Tina. How many did she have left?

Student's Name _____ Date _____

PROBLEM

Mr. Smith has a jar of jellybeans on his desk. How many jellybeans are in the jar?

1. The number is less than 30.
2. You say the number if you count by 5s.
3. The number is more than 10.
4. You say the number if you count by 4s.

Student's Name _____ Date _____

PROBLEM

Milton is standing in line, waiting to get into the movies. There are 5 people in front of him and 3 people in back of him. How many people are standing in line?

Student's Name _____ Date _____

PROBLEM

Reid and Raymond picked up a total of 20 cans from the playground. However, for every 2 cans Reid picked up, Raymond picked up 3. How many cans did each boy pick up?

Student's Name _____ Date _____

PROBLEM

Ann, Barbara, and Carol each have one coin: a nickel, a dime, or a quarter. Barbara's coin is worth the most. Ann's coin is worth more than Carol's. Which coin does each girl have?

Student's Name _____ Date _____

PROBLEM

Jan is making a necklace with paper shapes. She uses a pattern: 2 red circles, then 1 blue square, then 1 yellow triangle. Then she repeats the pattern. When she finished the necklace, she had used 5 blue squares. How many of each shape did she use?

Student's Name _____ Date _____

PROBLEM

You are making rock turtles. You need 1 large rock for the body and 5 small rocks for the head and legs. You have 10 large rocks and 25 small rocks. How many rock turtles can you make?

Student's Name _____ Date _____

PROBLEM

Mr. Elroy and his 3 helpers each make 1 duck decoy per day. How many do they make in a week?

Student's Name _____ Date _____

PROBLEM

The In-and-Out Sandwich Shop has 5 different sandwiches on its menu: tuna, turkey, hamburger, hot dog, and chicken salad. The Milou family ate at the Sandwich Shop twice last week. Mr. Milou ordered a tuna sandwich and a hot dog. Mrs. Milou ordered a hamburger both times. Eric had one turkey sandwich and one chicken salad sandwich. Mimi had a tuna sandwich and a hot dog. Maggie had a hamburger and a chicken salad sandwich. Which kind of sandwich was ordered most by the family?

Student's Name _____ Date _____

PROBLEM

The gum ball machine in Mr. Waldo's store has gum balls that are red, green, or yellow. Each gum ball costs 25¢. How many quarters do you need to be certain that you have 2 gum balls of the same color?

Student's Name _____ Date _____

PROBLEM

Tyler saw a truck, a car, and a bus go across the bridge. The car crossed the bridge after the bus. The truck crossed the bridge before the bus. In what order did the truck, the car, and the bus go across the bridge?

Student's Name _____ Date _____

PROBLEM

Each time the circus juggler appears in the ring, he adds to the number of balls he juggles. The first time he juggles 2 balls. The second time he juggles 4 balls. The third time he juggles 6 balls. If this continues, how many balls will he juggle the fifth time he appears?

Student's Name _____ Date _____

PROBLEM

To earn some extra money in school, Phil buys and sells old comic books. He buys them for 10¢ each and sells them for 15¢ each. How many comic books must he sell to earn 50¢?

Student's Name _____ Date _____

PROBLEM

Natalie has 2 quarters and 1 nickel. A candy bar costs 20¢. How many candy bars can Natalie buy?

Student's Name _____ Date _____

PROBLEM

A fence encloses a garden that is in the shape of a square. Each side has 4 posts. What's the smallest number of posts you need?

Student's Name _____ Date _____

PROBLEM

In a 3-person tournament, George scored 8 points. Ivan scored twice as many as George. Lynn scored 7 more points than George. Who was the winner and what was his or her score?

Student's Name _____ Date _____

PROBLEM

Maureen saves $1.50 a week to buy a video game. The video game costs $21.00 and she has already saved $6.00. How many more weeks must she save before she can buy the game?

Student's Name _____ Date _____

PROBLEM

Karl bought 10 tulip bulbs at 2 for $2.00. The bulbs usually cost $1.25 each. How much did Karl pay for the bulbs?

Student's Name _____ Date _____

PROBLEM

Justin works in the party store, filling helium balloons. Mrs. Adams ordered 70 balloons, some blue and some silver. She wants 20 more silver than blue. How many of each should Justin inflate?

Student's Name _____ Date _____

PROBLEM

Pam and her mother went shopping. She spent $18 on a new blouse and $7 for a hat. She then spent $5 for a scarf and $12 for a new purse. If she had $5 left, how much did Pam start with?

Student's Name _____ Date _____

PROBLEM

Greg has 36 baseball cards. His sister Rhona has 24. How many cards must Greg give to Rhona so that they each have the same number of cards? How many cards will each have?

REPRODUCTION PAGE 61

Student's Name _____ Date _____

PROBLEM

The monorail that rides around the zoo is 84 feet long. It has 4 cars, each 18 feet long. What is the distance between each car, if the distance between the cars is the same?

Student's Name _____ Date _____

PROBLEM

Simone bought 5 audiotapes from her tape club. The price of each tape is the same, and there is a $3.00 handling charge for the entire order. Her total bill was $23.00. What was the price for each tape?

Student's Name _____ Date _____

PROBLEM

At a local amusement park, the "Big Pelican Revue" takes place 4 times each day. The theater has 220 seats. Last Friday, 815 people saw the revue. How many empty seats were there last Friday?

Student's Name _____ Date _____

PROBLEM

The charge for renting a rowboat is $5.00 per hour for each of the first two hours, and $3.00 for each additional hour or fractional part. Louise and Rose rented a rowboat at 1:00 P.M. and brought it back at 5:30 P.M. How much did it cost them?

Student's Name _____ Date _____

PROBLEM

There are 6 children seated around a table in a cooperative learning group. Their names are Alice, Bob, Carol, Dennis, Edward, and Fran. Their teacher, Ms. Chang, has 50 multiple drill cards. She passes them around the table until they are all gone. Alice gets the first card, Bob gets the second, and so on. Who gets the 50th card?

REPRODUCTION PAGE 66

Student's Name _____ Date _____

PROBLEM

The local chess club is holding a "round-robin" tournament with 5 players. Each player plays one match against each of the other players. How many chess matches will be played in the tournament?

Student's Name _____ Date _____

PROBLEM

Maury is putting his blocks into a set of toy trains. He builds the first three trains as follows:

If he continues in this manner, how many blocks will be needed for the sixth train?

Student's Name _____ Date _____

PROBLEM

Lauren went to the Amusement Park on Tuesday. She bought tickets for two rides. She gave the ticket seller a $10 bill and received $3.75 in change. What two rides did she buy tickets for?

White Water Raft	$3.50
Hi-Bump	$3.00
Water Slide	$2.75
Tubing Ride	$2.00
Kiddy Shower	$1.00

Student's Name _____ Date _____

PROBLEM

Douglas and Seth are both working part time at the local pizza shop. Douglas works 1 day and then has 2 days off. Seth works 1 day and then has 3 days off. If they both work on March 1, on what other days in March will they both work?

Student's Name _____ Date _____

PROBLEM

The faces of a cube are numbered in order. Part of the cube is shown in the figure below. What is the sum of the numbers on the faces of the cube?

Student's Name _____ Date _____

PROBLEM

Jeff, Amy, Nancy, and Dan have formed a club. The club needs a president and a treasurer. They decide that each month they will change positions until all possible combinations have been used. How many months can they do this before they must repeat?

Student's Name _____ Date _____

PROBLEM

Four girls are waiting in line to buy tickets to the ball game. Charlotte is between Dominique and Vicki. Loretta is last in line, next to Dominique. Who is first in line?

Student's Name _____ Date _____

PROBLEM

Four friends went into a local ice cream parlor. Each ordered a different flavor: vanilla, chocolate, strawberry, and butter pecan. Aaron doesn't like vanilla. Kari's brother ordered vanilla. Kari cannot eat nuts because they stick in her braces. Barry handed the chocolate cone to Dolores and kept the vanilla cone for himself. Who ordered each flavor?

Student's Name _____ Date _____

PROBLEM

William and Hillary are shooting darts. William has already scored 17 with his 5 darts. Hillary has shot 4 of hers, and hit the target as shown. What must Hillary score on her final dart to beat William?

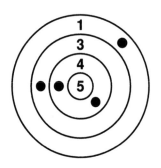

Student's Name _____ Date _____

PROBLEM

A firefighter is standing on the middle rung of a ladder. He moved up 7 rungs on the ladder, but the smoke got too heavy so he stepped down 11 rungs. When the smoke finally cleared, he went up the 17 remaining rungs to the top of the ladder. How many rungs are on the ladder?

Student's Name _____ Date _____

PROBLEM

Aleksi brought a bag with 36 oranges home from Florida to give to his neighbors. He gave one neighbor 11 oranges, a second neighbor 9 oranges, and a third neighbor 7 oranges. If he continues giving the oranges away in this manner, how many neighbors will receive oranges?

Student's Name _____ Date _____

PROBLEM

Pablo, Quentin, Ronald, and Steve are in an elimination tennis tournament. Pablo lost to Steve in the first round. Ronald played Steve in the second round. Ronald won one match and lost one match. Who won the tournament?

Student's Name _____ Date _____

PROBLEM

Tasha buys and sells baseball cards as a hobby. Last month, she bought some rookie cards and paid $3 for every 5 cards. Later, she was offered $3 for every 4 cards. She sold them all and made a profit of $9 on the entire lot. How many rookie cards did she buy and sell?

Student's Name _____ Date _____

PROBLEM

The indoor soccer league started the season with three teams: the Roaches, the Scorpions, and the Tarantulas. Each team played 1 home game and 1 road game against each of the other teams.

    a. The Roaches never beat the Scorpions.
    b. The Tarantulas never lost a home game.
    c. The Tarantulas lost 2 games.

Find the win-and-loss record for each team.

Student's Name _____ Date _____

PROBLEM

Lion cubs were born at the local zoo last week. The zookeeper weighed them two at a time, and got weights of 13, 14, and 15 pounds. How many lion cubs were there and what was the weight of each cub to the nearest pound?

REPRODUCTION PAGE 81

Student's Name _____ Date _____

PROBLEM

At the drugstore, Sondra can buy 1 postcard for a nickel, or 6 postcards for a quarter. What is the least it will cost her to buy 21 postcards?

Student's Name _____ Date _____

PROBLEM

Harry and Ezra entered a Walk-a-Thon to raise money for charity. They each had 10 people pledge $1.25 for each mile they walked. Together they earned $250 for the charity. How many miles did they walk altogether?

Student's Name _____ Date _____

PROBLEM

Juanita reads at the rate of 20 pages in 30 minutes. She is now on page 235 of a book that ends on page 345. How long will it take her to complete the book?

Student's Name _____ Date _____

PROBLEM

The auditorium in the town concert hall is organized by color-coded sections. One-half of the seats are in the blue orchestra section. One-fourth are in the red side section. One-eighth are in the green balcony section. The remaining 5 seats are on the stage side. How many seats are in each section?

Student's Name _____ Date _____

PROBLEM

Stacey and Bill have 3 pet dogs: Flaky, Shadow, and Lady. Flaky and Lady together eat 1 1/2 cans of dog food each day, whereas Shadow eats 3/4 of a can each day. If dog food costs $1.30 a can, how much do Stacey and Bill spend on dog food for a 4-week, 28-day period?

Student's Name _____ Date _____

PROBLEM

The Road Clearing Company is preparing a mixture of salt and sand to be spread on the roads this winter after ice storms. For every pound of salt, there are 3 pounds of sand. The truck holds a total of 2,000 pounds of the mixture. How much salt is in the truckload?

Student's Name _____ Date _____

PROBLEM

On a softball team, a "battery" consists of a pitcher and a catcher. The local team has 6 pitchers and 2 catchers. How many different batteries can the manager put on the field?

Student's Name _____ Date _____

PROBLEM

Melanie is paid by the digit when she uses her calligraphy skills to number the pages in a memory book There are 99 pages to be numbered. How many times will Melanie write the digit 7?

Student's Name _____ Date _____

PROBLEM

Alex, Helen, and Martha are giving a surprise party for their friend, Mai. They decide to share the expenses equally. Alex spent $35 for a gift, Helen spent $26 for the food, and Martha spent $20 for the decorations. What should they do for each to have spent the same amount?

Student's Name _____ Date _____

PROBLEM

Mr. Reynolds bought 8 gerbils to give the two kindergarten classes. How many different ways can he distribute the gerbils to the two classes?

Student's Name _____ Date _____

PROBLEM

Mrs. Lyons bought some prizes for her students. She spent $88 altogether on books and audio cassettes. Each book costs $7.00, and each cassette costs $4.00. She bought the same number of each. How many books did she buy?

Student's Name _____ Date _____

PROBLEM

During the family reunion, some members of the Hoffman family decided to go to the zoo. There were more children than adults in the group. They paid $90 for admission. The zoo charges $9 for children and $12 for adults. How many children and how many adult were in the group?

Student's Name _____ Date _____

PROBLEM

Workers in a store use the same legs to assemble 3-legged stools and 4-legged chairs. Last week, they used 34 legs. How many of each did they make, if they assembled more stools than chairs?

Student's Name _____ Date _____

PROBLEM

Two boys are paddling a canoe. They leave the dock at 9:00 A.M. and paddle downstream at 6 miles per hour until 11:30 A.M. Then they turn around and paddle upstream at 4 miles per hour until 2:00 P.M. Where are they in relationship to the dock?

Student's Name _____ Date _____

PROBLEM

The Pizza Shop sells two different sizes of pizza. A regular pizza that is 10 inches in diameter costs $6. The large pizza is 14 inches in diameter and costs $10. Which is the better buy?

Student's Name _____ Date _____

PROBLEM

A pet store has just received its monthly order. It received 40 more gold-fish than ferrets. It received 60 birds. It got 10 fewer canaries than goldfish. It received 20 parakeets. How many pets did the store receive in all?

Student's Name _____ Date _____

PROBLEM

The agricultural school garden is rectangular in shape and measures 20' × 45'. The students plant beans in 2/3 of the garden. One half of that contains lima beans. How many square feet of the garden are planted in lima beans?

Student's Name _____ Date _____

PROBLEM

Mr. Larson challenged his sixth-grade class to find how many different ways the students could make change for a 50¢ piece, without using pennies. How many different ways were there?

Student's Name _____ Date _____

PROBLEM

At the comic book show, Ursula is putting up her display. On the top shelf, she puts 1 *Superman* comic book that she sells for $10.00. On the second shelf, she puts 3 *Batman* comic books that sell for $5.00 each. On the third shelf, she puts 6 *Captain America* comic books. On the fourth shelf, she puts 10 *Spiderman* comic books. If she continues in this way, how many comic books will be on the seventh shelf display?

Student's Name _____ Date _____

PROBLEM

A candy bar is cut into equal pieces. Brittany eats 1/4 of the pieces. Then Nicole eats 1/2 of what is left. Finally, Anthony eats the last 6 pieces. Into how many pieces was the candy bar originally divided?

Student's Name _____ Date _____

PROBLEM

Roger spent one-half of his savings to buy a skateboard. Then he spent $12.50 for knee pads and the remaining $25.00 for a helmet. How much did he pay for the skateboard?

Student's Name _____ Date _____

PROBLEM

Ron has a rectangle with a perimeter of 30 inches. He divides it into 2 congruent squares. What were the dimensions of the original rectangle?

Student's Name _____ Date _____

PROBLEM

The roustabouts are setting up a circular pen for the coming rodeo. The fence consists of a set of posts and two 8-foot cross-rails between each pair of posts. The company ordered 40 cross-rails. How many posts will they need?

REPRODUCTION PAGE 104

Student's Name _____ Date _____

PROBLEM

David and Claire played a game in which the loser pays the winner 5¢ each time. When they had finished playing, David had won 4 games, but Claire had 20¢ more than when she started. How many games did they play?

Student's Name _____ Date _____

PROBLEM

One hexagon has a perimeter of 6 inches. Two hexagons placed side by side have a perimeter of 10 inches. Three hexagons placed side by side have a perimeter of 14 inches. (See the figure below.) What is the perimeter of 8 hexagons placed side by side in a similar fashion?

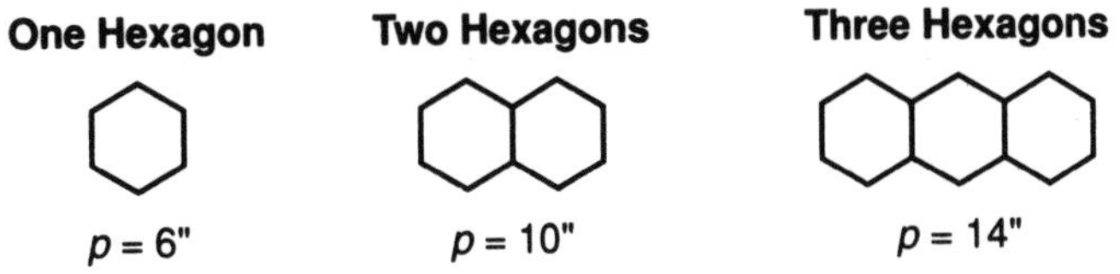

One Hexagon

$p = 6"$

Two Hexagons

$p = 10"$

Three Hexagons

$p = 14"$

Student's Name _____ Date _____

PROBLEM

Lou has collected 150 insects for his science project. He has exactly one-half of what he needs. Colleen is giving him 15 additional insects. How many does he still have to collect?

Student's Name _____ Date _____

PROBLEM

Ray answered 20 questions on his social studies test. He received 5 points for each correct answer, but 2 points were taken off for each incorrect answer. Ray received 72 on his test. How many questions did he answer correctly?

Student's Name _____ Date _____

PROBLEM

The Sports Emporium is closing out their stock of fishing lures. They had 48 lures left in stock. On Monday, Timothy marked them down to $5.00 each and sold 1/2 of them. On Tuesday, he marked the remaining lures down to $4.00 each and sold 1/3 of them. On Wednesday, he marked the remaining lures down to $3.00 and sold 1/4 of them. On Thursday, he marked the rest down to $2.00 and sold them all. He had paid $3.00 for each lure. How much money did the store make or lose on the sale?

Student's Name _____ Date _____

PROBLEM

The school cafeteria offers a complete lunch for $2.00, consisting of an appetizer, a main dish, and a dessert. All the lunches come with a container of milk. Today, the appetizer is soup or juice. The main dish is a hot dog, a hamburger, or a slice of pizza. For dessert, you can choose pudding or apple pie. How many different lunches could you pick?

Student's Name _____ Date _____

PROBLEM

When the giant clock in the town hall chimes, each chime takes 1/2 second. There is a 2-second interval between chimes. Thus, when it is 4 o'clock, the chiming takes 8 seconds. At that same rate, how long will it take to chime at 8:00?

Student's Name _____ Date _____

PROBLEM

Lisa ate 1/2 of the mini-muffins in the refrigerator and her brother Lorenzo ate 1/4 of them. Finally, their mother ate the remaining 6 mini-muffins. How many mini-muffins did Lisa eat?

Student's Name _____ Date _____

PROBLEM

Two boys are paddling a canoe. They leave the dock at 9:00 A.M. and paddle downstream at 6 miles per hour. At 10:30 A.M., they turn around and start upstream at the rate of 4 miles per hour. At what time do they return to the dock?

REPRODUCTION PAGE 113

Student's Name _____ Date _____

PROBLEM

Mona has $20 less than Jasmine. Laura has $20 less than Mona. Together, all three girls have $87.00. How much does each girl have?

Student's Name _____ Date _____

PROBLEM

Mr. and Mrs. Cooper are each starting a new job. Mr. Cooper will start at $30,000 per year and will get a raise of $3,000 per year. Mrs. Cooper will start at $20,000 but will receive a $5,000 raise per year. When will their salaries be equal?

Student's Name _____ Date _____

PROBLEM

Arthur, Pete, and Jacob went into the arcade, each with the same number of tokens. After each of them had used 4 tokens, the total they had left was the same number as each had started with. How many did each person start with?

Student's Name _____ Date _____

PROBLEM

There are 210 books on a shelf. There are twice as many mathematics books as history books. There are 10 more science books than mathematics books. How many of each are there?

Student's Name _____ Date _____

PROBLEM

A cooking class baked a batch of cookies to sell at the school bake sale. They made between 100 and 150 cookies. One-fourth of the cookies were peanut butter crunch and one-fifth of the cookies were chocolate chip. What is the largest number of cookies the class could have made?

Student's Name _____ Date _____

PROBLEM

Georgette is a television repair person. She charges $40 for a service call, which includes up to 1/2 hour of work. She charges $30 for each additional hour or part of an hour. Yesterday, she made 3 calls, lasting 1 hour, 1 3/4 hours, and 2 1/2 hours. How much did she earn yesterday?

Student's Name _____ Date _____

PROBLEM

Brian collects golf balls that fall into the water trap on the golf course, and then sells them as practice balls. He found some golf balls in the morning and arranged them in a square array on his counter. That afternoon, he found 9 more golf balls and discovered that he could now arrange all the golf balls into a different square array. How many golf balls did he find altogether?

Student's Name _____ Date _____

PROBLEM

The side of an equilateral triangle is 3 inches longer than the side of a square. The perimeter of the square equals the perimeter of the triangle. Find the length of a side of each figure.

Student's Name _____ Date _____

PROBLEM

One-Eye Pete left the bank he had just robbed, at exactly 1:00 P.M. and headed due south on the trail toward the border at 40 miles per hour. One hour later, the posse started after him on the same trail, taveling at the rate of 60 miles per hour. The border is 100 miles from the bank. Will the posse catch One-Eye before he reaches the border? If yes, how far was One-Eye from escaping? If not, how far from the border was the posse when One-Eye crossed over to safety?

Student's Name _____ Date _____

PROBLEM

Judy and Maryanne made bracelets from beads. They sold some of the bracelets for $1.00, and half as many for $1.50. Altogether, they took in $87.50. How many of each type of bracelet did they make?

Student's Name _____ Date _____

PROBLEM

A fuel tank is 3/4 full. When the gauge reads 1/4 full, the owner has the tank completely filled with 600 gallons of fuel. How many gallons does the tank actually hold?

Student's Name _____ Date _____

PROBLEM

Kim sold 51 jars of her homemade jam in exactly 3 days. Each day she sold 2 more jars than she had sold on the previous day. How many jars of her jam did she sell on each day?

Student's Name _____ Date _____

PROBLEM

A circular swimming pool is completely surrounded by a walk that is 2 yards wide. The radius of the pool is 50 feet. Find the area of the walk. (Leave your answer in terms of π.)

Student's Name _____ Date _____

PROBLEM

A 6" square tray of cornbread can serve four people. How many 12" square trays would be needed to serve 32 people the same amount of cornbread per person?

Student's Name _____ Date _____

PROBLEM

Rachel takes all the marbles from her marble bag and finds that she can arrange the marbles to form a square containing 13 rows, each of which contains 13 marbles. She finds that she can also arrange them into two smaller squares, with each row of the larger square having 7 more marbles than each row of the smaller square. How many marbles are in each row of the two smaller squares?